Effective Leadership
in Voluntary Organizations

Effective Leadership in

Voluntary Organizations

HOW TO MAKE THE GREATEST USE OF
CITIZEN SERVICE AND INFLUENCE

Brian O'Connell

ASSOCIATION PRESS   •   NEW YORK

To the Volunteers

361
O18e

EFFECTIVE LEADERSHIP IN VOLUNTARY ORGANIZATIONS

Copyright © 1976 by Brian O'Connell

Published by Association Press, 291 Broadway, New York, N.Y. 10007

International Standard Book Number: 0–8096–1906–7

Library of Congress Cataloging in Publication Data

O'Connell, Brian, 1930–
Effective leadership in voluntary organizations.

1. Volunteer workers in social service—Handbooks, manuals, etc.
2. Associations, institutions, etc.—Handbooks, manuals, etc.
I. Title.
HV41.033   361   75–38810
ISBN 0–8096–1906–7

Printed in the United States of America
Designed by The Etheredges

Contents

Preface

The viewpoints in this book constitute some guidelines for making voluntary organizations effective instruments for citizen service and influence. They represent more than twenty years' experience in voluntary agencies. To pointedly share that experience and to put myself on the line in the definite expression of it, the first person is often deliberately used.

Many of the references relate to the American Heart Association and to the National Association for Mental Health. These are the two voluntary associations with which I've been employed. However, through assignments with various interagency committees and projects and through numerous volunteer jobs, I've been able to get to know the operations of many other voluntary groups.

My career interest has been the promotion of citizen involvement in public affairs. This book is one additional attempt to foster such essential participation.

Earl Warren, Jr., initially urged me to put some of my experience into print. His encouragement was counter-balanced by the persuasive admonition offered by John Gardner in his preface to *No Easy Victories* that persons in the world of action should not attempt to write books because they don't have the time to do it well.

The scales were tipped by Judge Warren's successors as presidents of the National Association for Mental Health —all of whom argued that this particular field of action might profit from the views of a practitioner. They also helped me to carve out and protect the small islands of time which became the stepping-stones for getting this complicated assignment done. For that encouragement and patience, and for the many good lessons they taught me, my gratitude to Geri Joseph, Jim Chapman, Irving Chase, Helen Wright, Linden Wheeler and Gerridee Wheeler.

As with most extensive projects in voluntary organizations, this one was a combined volunteer-staff effort. I've drawn on the encouragement and experience of so many of the Mental Health Association staff that to list all of them would sound like the *begats* from the Book of Genesis. Nevertheless, my gratitude goes to all.

I must list the persons who served as an informal committee of readers and advisors. My special thanks, therefore, to Arnold Barach, Paul Messplay, Dave McDonnell, Ruth Morse, Ann Brown O'Connell and Bill Perry, Jr. Peter G. Miller also served with this group and participated as an editorial advisor at several critical stages to help achieve clarity, continuity and readability.

My brother, Professor Jeffrey O'Connell of the University of Illinois Law School, deserves special mention for his gentle determination to get me to write a book and for his patient guidance once he was satisfied I would try. Robert Roy Wright, my editor at Association Press, softened my initiation into the complex world of publishing.

The National Board of the Mental Health Association also eased my way by allocating from their special Board Fund a small but terribly useful sum to cover all the incidental expenses—which really do add up.

It's appropriate in this International Women's Year that my biggest thanks should be reserved for two remarkable women. My secretary through much of this project was Nita McClary, who worked through all the successive editions and still managed to keep both them and me organized. She would insist, and I agree, that it's important to acknowledge the willing help she received from Barbara Boone, Bob Carter and Arlene Holmes.

Nita's contributions were surpassed only by those of my wife, Ann Brown O'Connell, whose helpful criticism was matched by her encouragement and patience.

But with all the acknowledgments for how very much I owe to others, it must finally be recorded that it was I who wrote the book. And that I am solely responsible for any errors of fact or interpretation that the book may contain.

B.O'C.

McLean, Virginia
June 22, 1975

The Meaning
of Volunteering

People who get involved with public causes often open themselves to frustration and disappointment, but—through it all and after it all—those moments of making change happen for the better are among their lasting joys. There's something wonderfully rewarding in being part of an effort that does make a difference. And there's something sparkling about being among other people when they're at their best.

When any of us take inventory of the meaning of our life, these special experiences have to be among the high points. Happiness is, in the end, a simple thing. Despite how complicated we try to make it or the entrapments we substitute for it, happiness is really caring and being able to do something about the caring.

In the community sense, *caring* and *service* are "charity" and "voluntaryism." As far back as the twelfth century, the highest order and benefit of charity was described by

Maimonides in the Mishna Torah: "The highest degree, than which there is nothing higher, is to take hold of a Jew who has been crushed and to give him a gift or a loan or to enter into partnership with him, or to find work for him, and then to put him on his feet so he will not be dependent on his fellow man."

In a world just thirty years removed from the slaughter of six million Jews, and still rampant with diseases and other indignities of the vilest form and breadth, there is room for concern and caring, charity and volunteering. Indeed, in this still young democracy there is total dependence on citizen determination to preserve the freedoms so recently declared and to extend them to all.

The problems of contemporary society are complex, the solutions more involved and the satisfactions more obscure, but the basic ingredients are still the caring and the resolve to make things better. From the simplicity of these have come today's exciting efforts on behalf of humanitarian causes ranging from equality to environment and from health to peace.

In the course of these efforts there is at work a silent cycle of cause and effect which I call the "genius of fulfillment," meaning that the harder people work for the fulfillment of important social goals, the more fulfilled they are themselves. Confucius expressed it by saying that "Goodness is God," meaning that the more good we do, the happier we are, and the totality of it all is a supreme *state* of being. Thus, he said, God is not only a Supreme Being *apart* from us, but a supreme state of being *within* us.

Aristotle, too, caught an important part of it when he said, "Happiness is the utilization of one's talents along lines of excellence."

A simpler way of looking at the meaning of service is a quotation from an epitaph:

What I spent, is gone
What I kept, is lost
But what I gave to Charity
Will be mine forever.

Whether we want to express the meaning of service in involved ways or prefer simpler forms doesn't really matter. It can be charity or enlightened self-interest or man's humanity to man. These are all ways of describing why people volunteer, why volunteering provides some of our happiest moments, and why the good that people do lives after them.

Foreword:
Who Volunteers?

We Americans are organizing to influence every conceivable aspect of our human condition. We are increasingly willing to stand up and be counted on almost any public issue. We organize to fight zoning changes, approve a bond issue, oppose or propose abortion, improve garbage collection, expose overpricing, approve water fluoridation, enforce equal rights, or to protest war. And in the process we raise money and votes for a staggering array of causes we believe in.

Today a far greater proportion of our population is involved in volunteer efforts than at any time in our history. In a study entitled "Americans Volunteer," the U.S. Department of Labor demonstrates how Americans are involved in volunteer service: "A new consciousness of domestic deprivation, the beginning of racial militancy, and a rising affluence that permits increasing leisure have recently induced considerable growth and change in the traditional picture of the volunteer. Witness the legions of youth and young adults who spend several hours every week in helping youngsters learn to read. One remarkable aspect of the change is that many customary recipients of the volunteers' service are now serving their own and their community's interests: the young, the old, the handicapped, and the poor are serving as volunteers themselves. There are: (1) more volunteers, (2) different kinds of volunteers, (3) different kinds of functions, and (4) different channels for the delivery of their services."

As added proof of this, the 1974 edition of "Americans Volunteer," which was issued just as this book was going to press, reports that volunteering continues to increase. Specifically "Americans Volunteer—1974" reports that between 1967 and 1974 the proportion of the adult population involved in volunteer activities increased 6 per cent, or from 18 per cent to 24 per cent.

In the *New York Times* columnist James Reston terms the change "The Quiet Revolution." He points out that "what is happening now is that the model for action established during the civil rights battles of the 1960's is beginning to be applied to other fields." In the same column he added, ". . . citizen groups are forming to protect the environment, improve their communities, to challenge the assumptions and priorities of their elected officials, to defend the average consumer from the commercial gougers, and to work in many other ways for the improvement of American life."

One of the most encouraging developments is that volunteering now includes every economic group. Participatory democracy—which had been the exclusive role of the upper classes and then of the upper and middle classes —finally has broadened to include all parts of society.

Why, then, in the face of all the evidence of caring and service, do we increasingly hear the lament that man's humanity to man is declining as a characteristic of the

American way of life? Indeed, it seems to be a dominant impression that volunteering is sharply down. The answer to this probably lies in a strong difference of opinion about who and what activities are to be considered within our definition of volunteering. Note that the Department of Labor report refers to *different* volunteers, *different* functions and *different* channels for delivering services. It is these differences which begin to explain the striking contrast between the view that volunteering is in a serious slump and the facts as stated in the comprehensive Federal study. Although there is clearly a wave of activism in this country, the citizens involved, and their causes and methods, are so different from what has been traditional in the field that people viewing it from a slightly older viewpoint don't see what's happening as *volunteering*. They still view volunteering in a conventional frame of reference, while the report reflects a new frame of reference altogether. All this is considerably more significant than merely curious or academic. It is important to know what we want to preserve and foster if our efforts to promote voluntaryism are to be useful.

The development of volunteering in America has now evolved through four principal transition and growth periods. During each, the degree and nature of volunteer effort have changed significantly.

• The first stage was during the period of colonization in the early days of our country when banding together was necessary for survival, with the church in its way and the town council in its own way having dominant roles in promoting man's humanity to man.

• The Civil War marked the beginning of the second stage which extended for almost three-quarters of a century into the 1930's. These years provided a significant transition from individual charity to organized voluntaryism. Many of the organizations generally identified with volunteering were established in the Civil War period.

These include the Red Cross, Young Men's Christian Association (YMCA), National Conference of Social Welfare (NCSW), Volunteers of America, American branch of the Salvation Army, Chicago's Hull House, the American Public Health Association, the National Tuberculosis Association, Boys' Clubs, the National Society for the Prevention of Blindness, the National Association for Mental Health, Boy Scouts, Goodwill Industries, the American Social Health Association, the Family Service Association of America, and the American Cancer Society.

For the most part, these organizations represented only tentative beginnings, with their relatively small groups trying to spark widespread citizen interest in significant problems. It is both fascinating and important to realize that at the beginning of World War I the combined annual income of all the voluntary health and welfare organizations listed above was less than $17 million—the amount raised by just the National Association for Mental Health alone in 1975.

During World War I, this second stage of organized citizen effort burgeoned and there emerged an increased need for properly organizing this help. As during the Civil War, this voluntary spirit was largely sustained into the postwar years for relief programs and for an increasing list of domestic issues. The American Hearing Society was formed in 1919; the Crippled Children and Adults Society in 1921; the American Foundation for the Blind in 1921; Planned Parenthood in 1922; and then a whole new wave of veterans' organizations.

The depression years were a time when thousands of local relief activities were established. During the 1930's, the Community Chest movement developed. It was during this period, also, that the balance of roles between government and voluntary activity began to be actively studied, and the multiplicity of private organizations began to be of concern. Almost overnight, charity and service had become big business and volunteering hit a numerical all-time high. But even then the time of the *Gentle Legions* was still to come.

• With the establishment of the "March of Dimes" in 1938, the third major transition and growth period for organized citizen participation occurred. From that point through the next twenty years, volunteer service, which had largely been the province of the upper classes, suddenly was open to Middle America. Philanthropy, which had previously been the role of the wealthy, gave way to the nickel-and-dime collections and payroll deductions which are now the cornerstones of American giving.

World War II and the postwar Forties and Fifties lent great impetus to this third stage of citizen participation by the very number of new agencies that were developed and the breadth of the causes they represented. This was a period of staggering growth in the numbers of nonprofit organizations and the people who rallied to them.

In the 1950's voluntary health and welfare organizations represented the greatest source of volunteering the world has ever known. For the most part, they were made up of new middle-class recruits who started with door-bell ringing or other fund-raising roles and quickly moved into leadership.

On the giving side, of the $8 billion deducted for charity on 1962 income tax returns, two-thirds was contributed by families with incomes under $15,000. This period in volunteering is increasingly known as the time of the "Gentle Legions," after the book of that title by Richard Carter, in which he describes the impact of the "March of Dimes" and the new wave of voluntary health agencies on American philanthropy and volunteering.

• Within just twenty-five years, however, we were to take our fourth and largest step in citizen involvement. In the 1960's, participatory democracy suddenly began to include all parts of society. It was a change which bewildered the old-time volunteers and staff and so totally upset perceptions, even of who the volunteers are, that many national and community leaders still have not or cannot acknowledge the revolution. They are concerned that the power structure as they knew it is no longer intact and they believe that if we could somehow re-create it and restimulate the city fathers to recognize their responsibility to care for community needs, things would somehow get back in balance.

Those who believe that volunteering is declining clearly don't accept as volunteers the people who are immediately interested in their own problems. In a meeting with an advisory council to President Nixon's Committee on Voluntary Action, I was shaken to hear the members expressing an extremely pessimistic view of the state of volunteering. When I told the group that I thought things were far better than they believed and used as examples the healthy degree of caring represented by students, blacks, welfare recipients, anti-war demonstrators and others, my colleagues remonstrated that it was not appropriate to include as volunteers the people who have an immediate stake in the outcome of their own volunteering. I referred to the Colonial Minuteman and said that, traditionally and practically, it is appropriate that a person serving his needs or protecting his own rights belongs—past, present and future—in the family of volunteers.

It is a mistake to refer to our heritage of volunteering as if to suggest that altruism was the only characteristic of our history of volunteer effort. On the contrary, our traditions of volunteering evolved from a combination of the religious spirit of man's humanity to man and a very heavy dose of mutual dependence and assistance. The Minutemen and the frontier families practised basic forms of enlightened self-interest in their forms of volunteering. To portray our history of volunteering as though it were related solely to goodness of heart may describe the best in our forefathers, but would not identify the widespread tradition of organized neighborliness which hardship dictated and goodness tempered.

Many of today's voluntary agencies and their leaders are struggling to go back to the good old days. With the power structure exploding to every corner of the community and society, it is a tormenting business to try to pull together a consensus so that some positive movement is achieved. It is understandable that many would want to return to the older, more orderly days. Unfortunately, this regression would represent a regrouping along outdated lines rather than making full use of the truly exciting multiplication of people and groups who care and who are prepared to do something about their caring.

Many do not agree with the issues and tactics of today's activists and almost everyone deplores illegal practices which infringe on the rights of others, yet all who are interested in citizen participation must cheer the fact that so many people today are concerned enough to express their caring, and that our freedoms continue to provide these opportunities.

Happily, we have moved by stages from the exclusive level of Lord and Lady Bountiful, through the period of the elite "400," through the years of a concentrated power structure, and are now beginning to recognize that participatory democracy is everybody's business. We owe a tremendous debt of gratitude to Dorothea Dix and her kind, and to the community fathers who served so many causes, but the grandest huzzahs should be reserved for the here-and-now when democracy has truly come alive with all the population joining in the traditions of service and reform. Today, anyone who cares and is prepared to do something about the caring can make a difference.

1.
Getting Organized

Whether you want to get a traffic light installed at a danger-ous intersection, obtain special education services for a child with learning difficulties, expose job discrimination, protest against the storage of nuclear materials, or foster brotherhood—where do you start? This applies to an indi-vidual trying to get a toehold as well as to an established agency moving into a new community or program.

WHERE TO START?

The two basic steps are getting some facts and finding some allies. For both, I recommend starting with your po-litical representatives. Better than anyone else, they know how the system works and who makes it work, and they usually will feel an obligation to listen and try to help. For example, they are most likely to know who else has a re-tarded child or is worried about zoning or is concerned with improving public education. Also, they are most likely to know who the doers are and to be able to put you in touch with some of them. They can often open doors in the government departments which deal with your idea, concern or project.

I don't pretend that touching base with your political representatives or government departments will necessarily produce results. It may only add to your frustration. They are, however, the most likely and common sources of information about the system and about potential allies. And sometimes you'll be amazed at how quickly your problem can be solved or at least relieved by your starting with the people who have the power, understand the system, and know their constituency. Usually the solution to your concern requires allies and perhaps a lot of them. The sessions with your political representatives for fact-finding will usually be the best starting ground for identifying others who share your concern or who have a capacity for leadership in such projects.

The next group of people I talk to are past officeholders and others who have run for office in the area. Holding office and running for office both require knowing an awful lot of people, and that knowledge is what you should quickly tap into. Incidentally, don't be afraid to make a cold approach. These people are political animals, usually easy to approach, and surprisingly eager to help a fellow citizen.

My third general circle of contacts involves religious leaders. I've often gone into a community absolutely cold and by visiting a priest, minister or rabbi, I have quickly identified people who share my concern and people who are real doers. Those contacts serve two purposes—I not only get the names of some likely helpers, but I get automatic entree. Very few people will not see you if on your call you indicate that Rabbi Bloustein or Father Kelly has referred you. Often the clergyman will make the introductory call himself. It's amazing how helpful people will be if you dare approach them and ask for help.

The fourth group I contact are the newspapers. Editors and reporters know what's happening and while usually not so free with their time as the other groups, they still are approachable and willing to help. This may also lead to a news item or even a feature story about the problem you've identified. Don't overlook the neighborhood weeklies, the ethnic papers, and the shopping throwaways. Their editors know the community and are often generous with their space. They are very likely to do a news story or give a free ad which will tell people who you are and what you are trying to do. Talk to the radio-station managers, too. They know their community and may be able to provide important leads, and, last but not least, they may take to your cause and give you air time. Publicity is a very important link to other people and to generating concern and action. In Chapter 11 I've provided some additional information about how to get coverage for your cause.

If there is a United Way organization in your community, talk to its president, and if it has an executive director, talk to him also. These people may not be able to embrace your cause, but they do know the community and the people who volunteer. Here, too, you may be surprised that, because of a new emphasis on helping emerging organizations, they may be able to provide funding. If your community has a Volunteer Service Bureau or Voluntary Action Center (VAC), talk to them. They are a likely source for volunteers and of knowledge about the community. Look to the consumer-oriented groups. If there's a Consumer's Council in your community or state, they will have had experience in helping new causes get a start. Though they may not be able to take on your project, they can provide good advice about local people and about getting things done.

Still another likely source of information and contacts is school personnel. School principals know a great deal about the people in their neighborhoods, and are usually willing to lend an ear and a helping hand. Go and talk to other people who have gotten something going. The cause may not be immediately related, but the experience probably will be. Any one of the above people or groups can usually tell you who started a school for the deaf or who succeeded in blocking a shopping center or who forced the county council to hold open meetings. These are the doers who have learned your community or state and who are almost certain to be sympathetic to the combination of your dedication and confusion.

You may find that it's important to go from door to door or to pass out flyers at a bus stop or shopping center, or you may want to get a "reverse telephone" directory from the telephone company or some business and call people in your neighborhood or in randomly selected neighborhoods to see whether you can generate interest. The basic point is that if you have a real cause, you can find allies, but it's going to take some determination, nerve and hard work.

- By learning the system and identifying allies, you will have taken the two basic steps to achieving change.

PULLING TOGETHER

Without knowing your particular project or concern it's hard to be very specific. However, there are some ground rules which usually fit.

- The first essential is to keep it focused. The more you research the problem and the more people you enlist, the larger the focus can become. People will want to come on board who will not be interested in your exact cause, but will join if you agree to broaden your effort to cover their concerns. Be careful not to be so eager to enlist allies that you lose your focus!

• The second rule would be to keep it simple. For example, don't immediately get involved in an elaborate legal process of incorporation, and don't use up exciting new talent in developing and debating bylaws. To the extent possible, point the energy toward getting some results. Unless absolutely necessary, don't start very many committees. On most matters your central group should act as a Committee of the Whole. As the operation grows, decentralization will be necessary, but a good rule is to respond to that only when there's no alternative.

• Keep action oriented. People are tired of going to organizations which seem to be caught up in maintaining themselves or which are too timid to really bite the bullet. Hopefully you will have enlisted people who want to make a difference in a specific area and if they sense and see that you and the operation are action-oriented, you'll hold the best of them.

• Anticipate that you're going to have friction. You will have brought together people who are action-oriented and many who have a real concern about the problem. You can't expect such people to be very docile. There will be times when it will be important to take a deep breath and recall my opening statement that people who get involved with public causes often open themselves to frustration and disappointment but—through it all and after it all—those moments of making change happen for the better are among their lasting joys.

• Keep in mind that you're probably a unique individual and probably a strong one. After you've pulled the group together, you have to be careful that your leadership doesn't dominate. Give others a chance to speak and to do. Keep very much in mind that the cause needs these people and you're going to drive them away if you're too overbearing. One of the frustrations you'll face is that it will probably be important to take some steps backward before moving forward. For instance, you may have done a lot of fact-finding yourself, and you'll assume that the group accepts all of this and is ready to move onward. That's not very likely. They'll probably have to cover some of that same ground for themselves. Therefore it will make sense to involve some of your original best sources of information in meetings of your group or to involve some of your people in appointments with your sources. People have got to feel that they personally have gained a grasp of the facts and have had a chance to sift them before they develop a commitment to the course of action.

- Involve the group in deciding the attainable goals and the methods for achieving them. There's a good deal more on this in the chapter on planning, but the basic rule is to involve the group in identifying attainable goals and agreeing tenaciously to stick to those. You'll find that at different stages your people will want to change strategy, expand unrealistically, or even retreat prematurely. Decide together what it is that needs to be done and how to go about it and then tear into that effort with absolute conviction and tenacity. Goals and strategy should be *very* specific. In your fact-finding stage pin down exactly what has to happen to bring about your desired result and how you can make that happen.

- Don't assume you have to go it alone. You may well uncover other groups or services with which you can join to achieve your result. You may find that the best and most immediate course to follow is to go the route of the courts. You may find that your federal or state constitution or local charter or existing law already provides the protection or mandate you seek. Increasingly, citizens are suing their public officials to require implementation of existing laws or to extend and protect the rights of citizens. Your lawyer friends can tell you where to locate a public interest attorney or other lawyer willing to take on your cause.

• You will have to decide what your best course or strategy should be. You can picket, boycott, expose, sue, establish, elect, fund, lobby, shame, demonstrate, augment or whatever else will bring about the change or service you seek. The more specific you can be in defining the problem, goal and strategy the more rapidly you'll see results.

• If it's likely to be a long-term effort, condition yourself and the group to keep the faith. John Gardner has observed that "the first requirement for effective citizen action is stamina." It's almost certainly not going to be easy. For that reason it's essential to latch on to every evidence of progress and to be sure your members are given full opportunity to know that the effort is getting somewhere and that they have the right to be encouraged and to rejoice in the evidence of their growing power.

• Money will probably be important. The chapter on fund raising in this book deals with the problem of getting a new campaign under way. Also, there's a chapter on what fund-raising categories or activities you should consider. I won't repeat that information here, but I will state that people are very generous toward important public causes. You have the encouragement of knowing in advance that if you are really willing to work at it, you can raise the money necessary to start and sustain your endeavor.

BUILDING THE ORGANIZATION

Many of today's exciting voluntary efforts involve short-term projects to deal with immediate problems.

Neighbors or other fellow citizens spontaneously band together to deal with the problem at hand. This characterization of "ad-hocracy" is one of voluntaryism's best attributes. Unfortunately, though, there are many problems which just are not that amenable to early solution. For example, tackling mental illness or racism, or even undertaking to establish special education classes for retarded children, requires sustained effort. In turn, such efforts depend on a great many volunteers working together in a systematic way. When a good-sized army is needed, then a conscious effort has to be devoted to building the organization. Most organizations gravely underestimate this and their voluntary operations are generally chaotic. Building the organization begins with training the current leaders so that they recognize the need to devote time and resources to increasing the capacity of the operation. This may seem easily done, but it's usually not done at all. The early leaders are so impatient to be on with the crusade that they assume everybody feels the same fervor, and knows instinctively what to do. An organization's leaders must be made to see the necessity of building the organization to match their goals and they must be helped to learn how to do it.

In orientation sessions for volunteer and staff leaders, I use a two-part presentation entitled "Achievements Worth Building For" and "Building for Greater Achievement." This provides an opportunity to present the exciting accomplishments we can achieve while at the same time making clear that the achievements will be realized only if the leaders build an effective organization capable of such fulfillment.

One of the basic mistakes made in organizations is to automatically recruit as leader the expert on the subject without regard to his or her organizing skills. We eagerly recruit people to do organizing jobs for which they may be utterly incapable. If we want to organize a community program to reduce the incidence of stroke, we tend to seek out the cardiologist most experienced with vascular accidents. If we want to organize an advisory board to a community mental health center, we look for psychiatrists and clinical psychologists. If we want to organize a local chapter of the Cancer Society, we look for a radiologist. Experience instinctively leads me away from such experts as chairpersons or presidents and toward people with organizing skills. While the experts should be an important part of the committee, they are not likely to have the necessary organizational skills. Also, they may intimidate or otherwise turn off the very cadre of people whose enthusiasm and activity they should be building.

When setting out to recruit people, our approach is generally characterized by "get as many as we can—the more the better." The unfortunate result of this enthusiastic free-wheeling is that the recruiters almost always are overly optimistic, and when their accomplishments begin to fall far short of aspirations, the whole effort tends to crumble. Instead, figure out how many people are needed and cautiously predict how many of this number can be recruited in the first six months or the even first year. Do it *realistically.* Set *realistic* targets. Then divide the workload so that no one person is given an assignment in which failure is almost inevitable. Beware of the individual who wants to impress the group with how much he's going to do or how many cards he's going to take or how many friends he's going to sign up. A group which goes at building in a deliberate, realistic way (and this doesn't preclude fervor and determination) will be a lot farther ahead at the end of a year than one put together by optimists who assume their enthusiasm will carry the day.

Numbers are important, but so are the right people.

Identify who you need on your side to really put together the facts and the strategy and who will have the capacity to put that strategy to work. There will be times when you won't want people who already occupy seats in the power structure because they represent the status quo and that's what you want to change. Do not assume that you can't get somebody and move ahead to form a committee of lesser impact. Identify the people or at least the types of positions you need, and launch an effort to get the right persons to join you. You'll be surprised at how often they'll say Yes or lead you to other good people.

Effective people turn down appointments not because they are uninterested, but because the assignments are put to them in such a vague way that saying Yes could lead into a bottomless pit of responsibility. Too often we ask a person to come aboard without making clear exactly why we want him or her and without breaking the task down into reasonable proportions. If you want a member of the school board to join a committee looking at special education, ask him or her to sit in on those committee meetings that will include this topic. We make a horrible mistake in assuming that, in order to be effective, someone has to join the committee or board, when we are likely to enlist more of the right people by involving them only in the bite-size ad-hoc assignments for which they are really needed.

Recruiting also involves enthusiasm. People have got to know by your very approach that this is something you believe in and that it really does merit their time and attention. People want a cause—even busy people are willing to be further involved if they feel their service will make a difference. Don't assume that people already know about the cause. (This applies even to persons who have already been serving on committees or as members.) When you go to recruit someone for a key job, take the time to be sure he or she knows about the cause. This is likely to give a more positive frame of reference and a feeling of being part of something that is worth while.

Break the job down into bite sizes and into specific assignments so that the individuals get a grasp of exactly what you want and are not frightened by the implications of the commitment. Let them know you will be around to help. There is nothing worse than coming out of a hard sell only to wake up and find the leader acting as if he or she has got the sucker and is off to other victories. You have a responsibility to assist this individual to do the very things you have been struggling to do in your own assignment, including deciding what's needed, identifying the sources of help, and recruiting people.

The greatest temptation in recruiting volunteers is to make the job sound easy. It's natural to be eager to get a Yes, but in the long run this deception will catch up with you. It is better to give the individual a fair picture of the assignment so that, when you get a Yes, you will know you've got someone who is committed to getting the job done. It is better to get a few No's than to end up with someone who isn't likely to produce and who can't be held accountable because there is no mutual understanding of what is to be done. There is nothing in this to contradict your opportunity to be enthusiastic. The best guideline is to keep in mind that you want to come out of your recruiting effort with an individual who knows what is expected of him and is eagerly looking forward to getting it done.

A common failing of voluntary organizations is that the leaders become so directly involved in projects that they don't leave enough time for cultivation of their subordinate leaders. They find themselves directly responsible for so many activities that they don't have any real time for the stimulation of the interest and involvement of their people. To the extent possible, leaders should resist being their own project and committee chairpersons, so that their efforts can be devoted to identifying the tasks which need this kind of effort and to recruiting and cultivating the individuals who will be responsible.

Orientation begins during the recruitment process. All of that same ground and much more will be reviewed when a person has signed on. This includes orientation to the cause, to the organization, and to the individual's job. Each needs special attention, and the effectiveness of these efforts will often determine whether or not the individual in fact succeeds. Orientation is too often dismissed by giving the poor individual an unbelievable amount of material which he won't read or won't understand. Think carefully about who your recruit needs to meet if he is to gain greater knowledge and enthusiasm about the cause, and set these appointments up either on a one-to-one basis or in small groups. The important thing is to put yourself in the place of the new person and figure out what it is that he or she really needs to know in order to increase interest and enthusiasm and effectively to fulfill the assignment.

In addition to initial orientation to the cause and agency, most volunteers should receive continuing orientation, so that they will constantly feel abreast of the agency's impact on the cause. Too often orientation, if done at all, is limited to the first couple of weeks, and then we assume individuals get all they need to know from their occasional contacts with the organization. Every committee meeting should begin with an orientation segment which provides the committee members with knowledge of major thrusts and activities of the organization. Too often we forget that a committee member has little knowledge of the organization beyond his own assignment. From this limited vantage point, he or she can hardly serve as an enthusiastic communicator to the outside world. The president or leader should use every communication channel possible to give the volunteers a continuing sense of the mission and activities of the operation. This is essential if the members are to know that their efforts make a difference. People want to feel part of an exciting cause, but they won't get that feeling about your organization unless you, as the leader, take time to think through what they need to know in order to do their jobs effectively and what it is that people would like to know in order to feel that they are part of an exciting endeavor.

People will stay with your effort if they have a feeling of real usefulness. This involves their perception that they are doing some good and a feeling that the agency does represent a cause worth devoting one's energy to. These factors, in turn, relate to the leader's responsibility *a)* to give people jobs that are accomplishable, *b)* to give them an awareness of the effectiveness of the good work the organization is doing, and *c)* every possible opportunity to learn that they are making a difference. Giving people responsibility commensurate with their abilities and levels of interest is also a key to retention. People are just as apt to walk away if they feel they are being underused as if they are being overused.

Recognition is an important part of feeling needed. Voluntary organizations should have deliberate arrangements for recognizing effective service. This should not only apply to awards but also to promotion.

Many a leader has been amazed to discover that people he had unfairly pegged at one level of output were capable of much more. An individual who has demonstrated faithful service and effectiveness at one level is a first source of leadership for higher levels of responsibility. This includes doorbell ringers or envelope stuffers who have worked faithfully and who too often are overlooked for other responsibilities. Promotion should include some deliberate turnover of top leadership. The emphasis ought to be on the development of an increasing number of persons who are qualified and interested in top leadership posts. This is where there should be some turnover rather than at the lower levels where people drop off because they are overused, underused, or not turned on.

A president who really feels that this is his or her cause will usually be willing to take another assignment that involves a particular need of the agency or is of particular interest to the president. If a president has done the job well, and particularly when a succession of presidents have done their jobs well, there will be a rich pool of leaders moving up through the structure. That's the ultimate sign of real success in building the organization.

2.
The Role of the President

Many presidents of voluntary organizations confide that they're often well into the job before they really understand what it's all about. This is a sorry state of affairs, particularly so because much of what a president's term will mean is represented by what is accomplished during the first months on the job. The planning, recruiting, orienting, training and other essential leadership functions have to be accomplished, and accomplished very early, if the operation is to have sensible direction and exciting thrust. It's toward the goal of earlier preparation that the following urgent suggestions are made.

Mr. or Mme. President, you are the person morally responsible for your public agency. No matter how inadequate you may feel on the job, or even if you have people to whom you can delegate, you are the person who is accountable to your fellow citizens for the expenditure of their dollars contributed to help your agency pursue its service to society.

One of the biggest problems for voluntary agencies, particularly those large enough to have a staff, is that the presidents do not really perform as presidents, usually because they exaggerate the role of the staff. Because this is such a significant failing of voluntary agencies, and because the effective fulfillment of the role of president makes such a fantastic difference in the thrust of an agency, I have separated the comments about the presidential role from the discussion of relative roles of staff and volunteers. The next chapter will deal with that second topic, but for now I want to try as hard as I possibly can to help presidents really grasp how important they are.

Even if his organization has staff, a president should step back to see his job in the perspective of an agency which does not have staff. It may assist you to understand your presidential identity and responsibility if you try, at least at an early stage and perhaps periodically during your term, to imagine what your task would be like if you did not have staff backup. In an unstaffed Parent-Teachers Association, for example, the president is responsible for the recruitment, orientation, stimulation, and follow-up of all committee chairpersons, and unless the president functions, the organization doesn't go anywhere.

Look at your own table of organization—you probably won't see any staff on it. These organization charts usually include the Board of Directors, Executive Committee, president, and committee chairpersons, and that's the way you should see your job. You are the president, and you've got to go through the basic steps required of the chief of any operation. You are the person most essential to the agency's performance and, as such, the basic leadership responsibilities rest with you. These responsibilities include planning, recruiting, motivating, coordinating and evaluating. A good deal of the specifics about each of these tasks is contained in the chapters covering those subjects, but I want to focus here on the unique leadership role of the president in each of them.

PLANNING

One of the real problems of larger voluntary operations is that planning drifts toward becoming a staff responsibility. Thus, the volunteers themselves aren't really deciding where the operation should be going, and as a consequence of this the volunteers don't feel the vital commitment necessary to fulfill ambitious plans. You, as president, have to bring planning back to the volunteer side. And, believe me, this is tough to do! Even the aspirations you have and, indeed, may have voiced in your inaugural speech are easily suffocated in the day-to-day crises and tasks that so easily absorb the time you give. As a result of the lack of planning, you, the president, become totally occupied with what the organization presents rather than having some real opportunity to accomplish the things you set out to achieve.

To remedy this, I sit down as early as possible with my incoming president, and I urge him or her to decide on the one, two or—at the most—three things that he or she wants most to have accomplished when the term is finished. Most presidents make the mistake of starting out with too many aspirations, hoping that somehow they can achieve all those exciting goals. Unfortunately, they don't really pin down what it will take to accomplish the goals. Then, because of the lack of focus and the press of immediate problems, the goals never get firmly identified in the organization's mind and rarely are accomplished. Many presidents look back with regret to the fact that they never really got their teeth into some of the things that seemed so important at the beginning.

I advise the presidents with whom I work not to have

too many aspirations. Instead, they should think hard about the things they really want to accomplish before the end of their term. If the goals themselves are realistic, then, despite all the other things that hit you, somehow you will reserve a portion of your energy and resources to move ahead on your special projects. But you have to plan. You have to decide now what it is you want your organization to have achieved a year or two from now. You've got to involve the Board of Directors in a shared commitment to that goal or goals, and then you've got to help the organization bear down to see that the project is accomplished.

It's important not to try to change too much. An organization can only sustain or survive so much upset. Too often a president wants to change too many things, with the result that the upset is destructive. In some cases total reorganization may be indicated, and this should be frankly reviewed with the board so that a basic decision can be made. If that's not the problem, then choose your areas carefully and concentrate on them. Thus you won't be creating additional problems of morale, suspicion or anger which will only stand in the way of your accomplishing the things you want to do. Another aspect of planning involves your own schedule. Be sure you have cleared your docket to give the job the time and devotion it needs and be sure your family and associates are aware of the commitment and what it entails.

RECRUITING

Too often the president leaves critical recruitment for staff to pursue. This doesn't do the job. *You,* as president, have to decide who it is you really want to assist you in accomplishing the things you want to do, manage the ongoing activities, and deal effectively with the crises which are the day-to-day fare of a vibrant voluntary agency.

Don't give in to the easy way out by just letting Joe have a fourth term, even though he hasn't been a very good chairman up to now. Don't just hope that Harry will be better in his second year than he was in his first. And don't let the fear of relationship problems stand in the way of doing what's right. These are things that an effective president of any good operation has to face up to, and unless you're willing to conscientiously undertake the job of recruitment of able people, the organization won't really aggressively move forward to fulfill your aspirations or even perform its public mission.

Carefully analyze the jobs to be done, and then spend a lot of time identifying the people qualified to do them. This is worth a good deal of your time early on or even in advance of your administration. It will not only save time later but it will mean the difference in how much progress is made. *Remember,* it is important to choose as project and committee chairpersons, individuals who are good organizers rather than people who happen to be experts on the subjects involved. Put the experts on the committee, but use good organizers as your principal subordinates.

MOTIVATING

Even after presidents have given realistic attention to planning and recruiting, they usually leave the rest to staff or to chance. Staff can carry a good share of the load of training, but your presence must still be felt. Your efforts in effectively involving your key subordinates in major activities and decision-making are essential. Keep in mind that these are your people. These committee chairpersons, project chairpersons, and your other officers are your subordinates. They want to know what *you* think . . . they want to know where *you* are going . . . they want to know how *you* perceive the organization . . . they want to know what *you* consider important to be done.

Most presidents assume that this kind of thing just happens, that the executive has somehow communicated all these things or that a past chairperson has oriented a successor or even that a person, simply by having been a member of the board, has a grasp of the new and larger responsibility. There can't be cohesion in the organization without your involvement in orientation and training and without your giving a great deal of thought as to how to effectively motivate, inspire and stimulate persons who will be carrying the major part of the load. Particularly, the organization can't be moving as a unified phalanx toward the goals set by you and the board unless your key subordinates have participated with you in deciding where the organization is going and really feel they are an integral part of the operation.

You've also got to be the regular motivator, encourager, and prodder. It's not sufficient that you might involve the subordinates in planning and assist in their orientation and training; you've got to provide regular opportunities for discussion of progress and problems. It's important to be on that phone five or six times during the year just to say, "Mary, how's it going? I heard about your meeting last week. I am sorry I couldn't get there, but I am delighted with what I hear about it. Is there anything I can do for you? We're putting you on the agenda of the Executive Committee meeting and we're really looking forward to that report. I hope we'll get the material well in advance, so everybody can enjoy it and act intelligently on it."

Don't assume that if you're regularly communicating with the executive director about things that you're really touching base with your own subordinates. They are human beings, and an organization will respond far better if you, as the human leader, are in touch with your human subordinates in a human way. If they feel you're really interested, they'll respond and they'll perform similarly with the people responsible to them, and the total operation will be many times stronger. Obviously it's important not to overlook the human need of people to have their backs patted and, in some cases, their bottoms spanked . . . and only the president can perform these functions.

An important part of orientation and training relates to your successor. As soon as he or she is identified, do everything possible to build toward a natural succession. The next president should be able to move in without too much effort and with minimum disruption to the thrust of the organization.

COORDINATION AND FOLLOW-THROUGH

It's your responsibility to see that the activities which the officers, Board of Directors and committee chairpersons set out to do are being done. One of the basic approaches is to have certain checkpoints during the year. At those times, provide project and committee chairpersons with an opportunity to report at meetings of the Executive Committee and Board of Directors. It will also be important to stay close enough to enable you to judge the progress or lack of it and to sit down with the chairpersons to discuss any impediments.

If a key subordinate is letting you down, face up to replacement. Usually the individual will be relieved to be out from under the responsibility. But even if he or she is unhappy with your action, your larger responsibility is to the contributors of public money and to your community.

To have time for basic management responsibilities, it will be essential for you to avoid being directly responsible for immediate projects. Find people who can carry these for you. Your function and goal is to see that the volunteer talent of the organization is being developed. To the end that you get trapped into responsibility for individual projects and issues, you will not be using your limited time to expand the capacity of the organization to deal with an increasing number of projects and issues.

Be fully conditioned to the human relationships aspects of the role of president. Be prepared and leave time for dealing with many different personalities, most of whom at some point will need soothing, stroking and encouragement.

EVALUATION

Your success will be measured in three important ways: 1. The achievement of the things you set out to accomplish. 2. Fulfilling the organization's other major projects and its response to the unexpected crises and opportunities. 3. The increased increment of volunteer involvement, leadership and responsibility which has been generated during your term.

Develop some regular checklist to gauge progress on the specific tasks set out at the beginning of the year and to measure increased volunteer activity. At mid-year sit down with some objective persons you can trust and take a hard look at the progress or lack of it. If you know that you're going to be doing this at various checkpoints, it will increase your determination to come off with good scores.

Over the years I've developed a list of what I call musts for presidents. I know that individual situations vary, and perhaps not all of these will fit your circumstances, but my general observation is that the president who rates well on this checklist will be running an exciting operation. On the other side, in the breakdowns I've seen of presidential leadership in voluntary organizations, the failures can usually be traced to ignoring some of these musts:

1. Decide in advance that your largest goal for the year will be to increase the degree of citizen involvement and responsibility within the organization.

2. Be the president. This leadership role cannot be delegated to the staff, and to the extent that you are confused about your leadership responsibility or to the extent that you turn over this role to staff, your success will be compromised by that much.

3. Involve your key officers and other subordinates, including staff, in a planning session to effectively determine where you as a team want to be at the end of your term. Be sure that these plans are realistic and attainable. Be sure that the Board of Directors has a final opportunity to approve them.

4. Approve all Board of Directors and Executive Committee agendas and make certain that these are sent out at least ten days in advance of the meeting. Much of what you will be trying to do as the leader of the organization will be lost unless these meetings of the Board of Directors and Executive Committee are *your* meetings and represent *your* checkpoints for progress toward the year's goals. It is essential that the agendas be sent in advance so thoughtful people can give thorough consideration to the issues.

5. Involve your key subordinates and keep in regular personal touch with them.

6. Appoint, orient, encourage, and follow-up on your project and committee chairpersons. If you leave that to the staff, it may be done but it won't be accomplished with the same degree of warmth that your personal contact supplies.

7. Plan regular meetings with your executive director, setting aside ample time so that you two can really get into some of the current issues and have enough time left over to check on progress or lack of it on the year's goals.

8. Plan for the annual evaluation of the executive director. Even if he or she is tops, small problems can com-

pound into large ones if there is not some process by which the volunteers can make observations and suggestions. Build it into the system that the Executive Committee or Board of Directors should do the annual evaluation and then set aside time for it.

9. Build positive relationships within the total organization. If your group is part of a larger organization, develop personal relationships with the volunteer leaders at the other levels. Try to do everything possible to minimize friction and to promote effective relationships.

10. Make it exciting and worth while. Keep in mind your unique position and opportunity to know what's going on in the organization. Provide regular occasions through board meetings, newsletters, personal communications, and every other possible way in order that your fellow volunteers can have the fun of being in the know and also have some feeling of being part of an organization that *is* making a difference.

11. One last must. Realize that *you* are responsible, and if you leave a void, it will be filled of necessity by the executive director, who thereby will become too influential and too preoccupied with doing your job to help expand volunteer involvement and impact. Don't worry about making the executive director too important. The greater danger occurs when you let us become too important at the expense of building volunteer responsibility.

This chapter has tried to give you a clearer perception of your identity and responsibility as president. If you have staff, your role is still the same—your goals will still be the same, your evaluation of your success will still be the same —but you will have skilled hands to help you fulfill your functions. The next chapter is intended to give you a further grasp of the relative roles of volunteers and staff.

3.
Volunteers and Staff: Who Does What?

When reviewing the role of the president in the last chapter, it was useful to try to see the president's job in the perspective of an agency without staff. It might be similarly useful here to take a look at a totally volunteer organization which comes to the point of needing and being able to afford staff.

IT'S A VOLUNTEER ORGANIZATION

It's my observation that most organizations go into a temporary downturn when staff is first hired. The pattern is fairly typical. A wonderful group of dedicated volunteers, through their own individual efforts and without staff backup, have scrambled, kicked and scratched their way to having a significant program so that they now feel they need and can afford some staff assistance. They hire a staff and immediately the volunteers relax, turning much of the work over to the staff director. The volunteers assume that the agency will not only carry on the existing activities but will now in fact be able to spurt forward.

In about a year, however, or at the most two, the volunteers begin to view the scene with bewilderment. They find that the agency is really doing less than it was before they hired staff and has lost much of its visibility and vibrancy. There will be a tendency on the volunteers' part to conclude that obviously the wrong staff was hired because more was being accomplished when the volunteers were doing it by themselves. Before the downturn and the discouragement become irreversible, the group's members may finally realize that they had turned over far too much of the job to the staff and retreated to occasional approvals of what the staff did along with some irregular assistance to the poor bloke who is president but who has been feeling less and less responsible for the operation.

The worst illusion ever perpetrated in the voluntary field is that which says the Board of Directors makes policy and the staff carries it out. This is just not so. The board with the help of staff makes policy and the board with help of staff carries it out. Unless volunteers are committed and involved in the action phase of the program, the organization cannot develop and, in fact, should not be characterized as a voluntary organization. Also, it is naive to assume that staff doesn't have considerable influence (usually too much) on policy formulation.

Staff exists to help the volunteers do the work of the organization. Staff should not be expected or allowed to do the job directly. The greatest sinner is often the president who far too often gives over responsibility to the executive director.

Most presidents and boards are not certain about the appropriate and relative roles of volunteers and staff in a voluntary agency. Whenever counseling with a president or a board it is useful to bring them back to the exercise of viewing the organization without staff so that all the volunteer responsibilities and functions can be clearly identified. Only after that's done do I reintroduce the availability of staff, making it clear that staff is hired to assist the volunteers to do their citizen jobs in fulfillment of the voluntary agency's mission.

PINPOINTING THE FUNCTIONS OF STAFF

There are two extremes in the concept of staff's role in voluntary organizations. The first identifies the staff person as the expert who acts principally in an advisory capacity to the interested volunteers. This interpretation is typified by the fund-raising consultant who is hired by a church or a hospital to show the volunteers themselves how to raise a stipulated sum of money. The second extreme identifies the staff person as simply the individual who carries out the clerical details of the agency's function. This interpretation is typified by the executive secretary hired by a service club to arrange details of meetings and handle routine correspondence. In vibrant citizen organizations the correct role rests squarely between these two. The professional staff person is no less an expert in the specialty than the church's fund-raising consultant, but neither are the staff functions dissimilar from the everyday activities which the service club secretary is performing of handling the routine business which the volunteers do not have time to process.

The reason most staff people must be experts and detail people at the same time stems from the nature and magnitude of the mission their organizations represent. Because they are probably working with staggering community or national problems, even the details of working out a program and launching it require the daily attention of a skilled community organization specialist. On the other hand, the staff member must be a detail person because he is dealing with a problem so comprehensive that no one expert can possibly cope with it. An intelligent attack requires the concerted action of many different specialists and community representatives who volunteer their time to determine solutions and pursue them.

Voluntary organizations are fortunate in being able to bring the thinking of many specialists to bear on the problems; but, in doing so, these citizen volunteers must be served with facts, with legwork, and with all the other details that go into making volunteer time pay off. To illustrate how this works in daily operation, we may take the example of a staff person working in the area of rehabilitation for the Heart Association. Basically, this person must be knowledgeable in the process of rehabilitation. He or she must know what has and is being done in rehabilitation elsewhere in the community and in the Heart Association, along with having a basic idea of what specialities are needed to properly attack the problem at hand. At this point, the job becomes a matter of feeding all necessary facts to the proper individuals so that the right committee is formed and can as quickly and efficiently as possible come up with the right program to meet the principal needs with which it is concerned. In a sense, the organization and the staff person are picking the brains of these volunteer experts, translating their thinking into a program plan that utilizes existing knowledge and services, working with a committee to modify that plan, and helping the committee to launch a program in the community.

In every sense, the rehabilitation staff person is servicing the committee with the facts, legwork, knowledge of the agency, knowledge of the community, plus an ability to translate the intentions of the volunteers into a plan and, in turn, into the kind of program which the thinkers themselves would inaugurate if the agency could ever afford such a full-time team. Having staff means the committee can be utilized to its maximum because the volunteers are not continually bogged down with details or lack of information. In an agency where volunteer leaders can give only limited time, the business of processing details and fact-gathering would mean indefinite delays if someone were not available to do this for the committee. With staff, the Rehabilitation Committee, instead of taking two years to develop and effect one program, can actually develop and undertake many programs in the same time span. The basic concept of staff assistance is to leave the *big* people free to think about the *big* things and then to give them sufficient assistance to translate their thoughts into *big* results. With this interpretation of the role of staff, the Heart Association is able to attract to the organization the important volunteers who will serve as the program force of the agency and the organization is making the most of the time they give.

A few years ago I collaborated with Geri Joseph, then the national president of the National Association for Mental Health, in order to put together a summary of what we as the chief volunteer and staff officer jointly considered to be the essential functions of staff. This is the way we framed the job:

"The role of staff in a voluntary agency is simple in concept (though certainly not in execution). Your job is to bring about the maximum *volunteer* dedication, *volunteer* involvement, *volunteer* responsibility, *volunteer* impact and *volunteer* satisfaction. You must stimulate, educate and service. . . . Everything you must do must be directly related to the single underlying concept of voluntaryism—the promotion of citizen interest in public affairs.

"To the extent you become project oriented and lose sight of your basic role of developing the *volunteer* capacity of your organization, we might just as well declare ourselves a branch of government. Your mission, your project, your goals and your record must be measured in quotients of *volunteer* commitment and *volunteer* results."

We then went on to list twelve functions staff can perform to make volunteers more responsible and active. These are abbreviated below:

• Set your annual goals not in terms of pursuit or completion of specific projects, but in terms of increased volunteer involvement and commitment.

• Provide all possible assistance to volunteers to help them understand the problems in this field and the role and work of this organization. Volunteers won't feel comfortable and therefore won't really give fully of themselves unless they are well informed and kept briefed on all relevant matters. That doesn't mean sending reams of material. A key part of your job is to summarize information so that it is understandable to volunteers.

• Provide excellent staff service to the president or to the committee chairpersons who rely on you for staff backup. Nowhere is this more critical than in the executive director's responsibility to the president. While the executive director is many things to many people, he is also the executive assistant to the president. He should see that the president has all the information he needs to fulfill his obligation as elected head of the organization. Don't do the president's job, but help him to understand that job in order to do it well.

• Provide the best possible service to other officers and to the board, committee chairpersons and committees. If there is one general failing of staff in organizations such as ours it is that staff somehow assumes that volunteers are mind readers, that they know the issues and facts. How often we go to committee meetings without the agenda and related details having been distributed in advance. And how often we simply listen to staff or an uninformed committee chairperson ramble on about some issue we don't understand, but which must be solved at that very meeting. If you care about the involvement of volunteers—quantity and quality—then be certain that every meeting is carefully preceded by a sharing of the agenda and all pertinent information at least a week in advance of the session. Then volunteers can think about the subject and come prepared to offer competent advice. You'll find people will be more willing to come to meetings, too. If you don't do this, however, many people will feel the organization is haphazardly run, and will not want to be part of hasty decision-making.

• Help identify the points of view and talent needed on the board and on the committees, and, to the extent necessary, help in the recruitment of such people. Leave as much of the job as possible to the president and committee chairpersons. And once these people are assembled, let them make the decisions. Don't try to have all the bright ideas. Your skills are needed in knowing the type of people who should be brought together and in giving them the right support. If a staff person—or, for that matter, a volunteer—assumes that he or she has talents equal to the composite brains and skills of a committee, then the organization either has a genius on its hands or, more likely, is in trouble.

• Your first program obligation is to know the facilities in your own area. Only to the extent that you really know what is already available can your volunteers help identify gaps, weaknesses and needs.

• Be certain your organization operates a competent information and referral program. This may seem a minor point, but the basic service activity of a volunteer agency is to serve as a channel between those who need help and those who can provide it. Too often a voluntary agency tends to wait for the glib, exciting projects when, in fact, its fundamental job is to fulfill the basic roles of gadfly, information and referral source, demonstrator, and so on.

• Put a priority on planning. Identify those basic things which need doing most, and then do them well. Despite the many temptations, don't spread yourself so thin that basic obligations and priority projects are not done adequately.

• Stay loose or at least stay flexible. The basic role of a voluntary agency is to see that whatever needs doing is, in fact, accomplished by whoever can do it best. This requires the *habit* of *flexibility*—two seemingly contradictory words—and an ability to move from one challenge to another. The role of staff is obviously to be responsive to the need for change.

• Recognize your role as the basic communication link in the organization. Because you represent continuity of service, you are the source of information on the past. You are also a key source of information about what is happening now in your community and in your organization.

• Keep the dream alive! Don't let yourself be so concerned with the problems you face that you fail to recognize the fact that volunteers look to you to keep the goals in sight. It is up to you to be certain that people are aware of the long-term goals and of the capacity of the organization to work effectively toward those goals.

• Provide all possible credit, thanks and satisfactions

for volunteer activity. This will require a good deal of subordination of your own ego, but your goal and your satisfaction must be in the degree and kind of volunteer effort achieved.

Of all of those points I'm quite certain that Geri Joseph and I would give first place to "Keep the Dream Alive!"

MAINTAINING THE DELICATE BALANCE

The most important job a Board of Directors does is hire the executive director. The next most important task is to see that the executive director is fulfilling the staff role in contrast to the volunteer role. The board must have the mechanisms by which it can be certain that the staff is not usurping the role of the board. While not denying the major role which the staff has in volunteer organizations, the basic problem is that in too many cases staff has really taken over.

It is essential that the Board of Directors, or at least the Executive Committee, should do an annual review of an executive director's performance. The review should be based on the job description and on the executive director's role in assisting the volunteers to carry forward the association's work. Most organizations overlook the need for an annual review and, in fact, no evaluation is done until a point of brinkmanship is faced. The performance of the executive director should be measured in relation to his ability to contribute to expanded volunteer involvement and responsibility. The evaluation should take up a substantial part of the time at an Executive Committee or Board of Directors meeting. Incidentally, I don't believe this critical responsibility should even be delegated to a Personnel Committee.

The review should not include evaluation of staff per-

sons other than the executive director. Though the evaluation automatically has to cover staff performance in general, the executive director should be given absolute authority for the annual evaluation of his staff.

Unless this matter is taken seriously, it will be given
only cursory attention. The Executive Committee should
take at least an hour, because it takes time before the members feel comfortable and will discuss shortcomings. Even
if the executive director's performance is tops, it's still important that small problems be caught before they com-
pound into large problems.

I predict that most evaluations will follow this pattern.
For the first few minutes there will be silence. For the next
ten minutes there will be laudatory statements, such as
"Boy, he works hard" . . . "Wow, does he work hard"
. . . "Gee whiz, he puts in the hours." After about twenty
minutes someone will finally raise a point, such as "I know
he works hard, but I'm not sure what he does all that time."
The session obviously should not be nitpicking, but it
should be thorough enough so that if members have concerns about performance, these can come out and be objectively discussed. At times this process indirectly solves
other relationship problems. A member of the Executive
Committee may be laboring under a misconception about
the executive director's role or handling of a given situation and once it's brought up the misunderstanding may be
dispelled. The president should take time after the meeting
to review the report, including items of commendation and
areas for improvement.

Generally, staff evaluations, whether *of* the executive
director or *by* the executive director, should not take place
at the same time as a salary review. Ideally, the two should
be about six months apart. The situation just gets too
highly charged if the evaluation has an immediate transla-
tion into salary considerations.

Although the executive director should have absolute authority over other staff within the organization, the Board of Directors will exercise ultimate control by its authority to approve the personnel policies and practices of the organization, including the wage and salary administration program. The board must also have firm authority for the basic table of organization—that is, the executive director should not be free to make significant changes in the deployment of staff without the staff organization chart being approved by the board. This is a gray area where staff and board often clash. To me, however, it's an inviolate rule that the board must have authority to pass on the staff structure. The way the staff is organized and the job descriptions carry such influence on future directions and activities that the board must have the principal responsibility for their determination.

In my own experience, when I began to think about significant reorganization of the Heart Association staff in Baltimore I went to the Executive Committee and outlined the reasons I felt change was necessary. We then had a good deal of discussion as to whether my basic idea had merit and I was encouraged to develop a more detailed plan. That initial discussion helped clarify and even changed some of my thinking. I then brought a plan to the Executive Committee and to the Board of Directors for their reaction and for discussion. On the basis of those two presentations, I developed a final report which was approved by the Executive Committee on authority from the Board of Directors. Once that plan was approved, it was entirely mine to implement with whatever individuals I chose to recruit, assign or promote.

This was my approach also with two reorganizations of the National Association for Mental Health staff.

The board should also be heavily involved in development of one-year and five-year plans and in the evaluation of the annual fulfillment of those plans.

An area of frequent difficulty in board and executive director relations involves the degree to which the executive director serves as the spokesperson for the agency. In some agencies the executive director becomes the public spokesperson by default. In others the board deliberately wants the executive director to be "Mr. Outside." Generally it is consistent with the ideal of promoting citizen responsibility and influence that the executive director should be much more "Mr. Inside," and the public exposure should accentuate the volunteer face of the organization. The president should generally be the spokesperson. If the topic involves a specialty area, then the volunteer covering that area might speak.

It's important, too, that the organization in other ways have a true volunteer characterization. It's a good idea to have volunteers representing the organization whenever possible. Staff are often tempted and eager to accept assignments which take them away from their own jobs and which hide the volunteer face of the agency. Staff people should resist almost every opportunity to represent the agency in the community. Too many times the executive director, because it's the easiest way or because he or she is fascinated by it, will become the association's representative on the community council and on many other advisory committees and boards. An executive director does not belong on any of those committees unless there is some unique factor calling for staff input. Those responsibilities belong with the volunteers because without these exposures the agency isn't really functioning as a volunteer organization. If the volunteers aren't getting this kind of experience, they are not gaining the satisfactions, the encouragement, and the insights which they need in order to expand their capacity to be better leaders of the organization.

Personally I resist the most tempting invitations to serve on fascinating national boards and committees and to participate in exciting national and international conferences. I turn down every one of these no matter how tempting and no matter how time-consuming it may seem to be to find the right volunteer to replace me. Once volunteers are filling these roles they will have much greater satisfaction in being part of the organization and their reports are much better received because it isn't always the executive director telling the board about this and that.

In too many cases the staff finds itself so burdened with outside assignments there isn't time to do the basic inside staff jobs. It's essential that the executive director should not become your "Mr. Mental Health Association" or "Ms. Red Cross." This happens so easily and so quickly that it's necessary to be always on guard against it. The last chapter ended with the admonition to presidents that they must not leave a void in leadership because it will be filled, of necessity, by the executive director, who will thereby become too influential and too preoccupied with doing the president's job. This is a fair warning for all volunteers and it is worth repeating that the board should not be too worried about making staff important. The greater danger is in letting staff become too important at the expense of building volunteer responsibility.

STAFF IS NOT OVERHEAD

This chapter began by exploding a myth that volunteers make policy and staff carry it out, and it can end by dispelling another myth. Too often people think of staff salaries as an overhead expense and even some fairly sophisticated boards become concerned if staff salaries begin to represent a high proportion of the budget. Contrary to this, I frequently counsel boards that unless the staff salaries and other supporting expenses come above 50 per cent of the budget the agency probably is not doing a real job.

The basic program force of most citizen organizations is in the volunteers' time and energy which moves the community toward improved attitudes and practices, but keeping volunteers vibrantly active requires staff backup. The major cost of operating most voluntary agencies is the staff which provides day-to-day service to the volunteers. The staff person serving a childhood-mental-illness committee or working to promote jobs for the handicapped or a minority group is every bit a program expense as is the nurse in a hospital, teacher in a school, or minister in a church. I certainly agree that overhead should be kept as low as possible and that if the staff is spending most of its time on fund raising or management activities, there is need for concern. But if the staff time is logged on behalf of the mission of the organization, it is program money well spent.

4.
Recruiting the Right Staff

Selection of the staff head of an agency is clearly the most important decision a board makes. In turn, staff selections by the executive director have a tremendous bearing on the success of the operation. For these reasons and because staff recruitment is handled inadequately so often, the subject of staff recruitment deserves a chapter of its own.

PROFILE OF THE SUCCESSFUL STAFF PERSON

It's increasingly my experience, born of many sad lessons, that it takes a unique person to succeed in the staff role in a voluntary agency. This doesn't mean that successful staff people are better than other people, but they clearly are a different breed of cat. Over the years, I've evolved a profile which helps me screen persons who are exploring staff possibilities. My current profile of the persons most likely to succeed is as follows:

- *They're committed to public service.* This is more than a generalization. The persons who succeed will face many rocky times. They'll be underpaid for their ability and they'll put up with a great deal of conflict. For these reasons and many more, these persons must have a dedication to public service which will drive them through and over these obstacles and tough times.

- *They like people and get along well with them.* Liking people is too often used as the only criterion for selection and therefore it can be exaggerated. In carrying responsible positions in voluntary agencies, however, most staff people deal with a wide variety of individuals and must be able to get along with them.

- *They can subordinate their personal needs and preferences to the needs and goals of the volunteers.* This is among the characteristics which screen out the majority of people. Most of us cannot consistently subordinate our needs, aspirations and satisfactions. But the really successful staff persons in the volunteer agency must have this capacity or otherwise competition between staff and volunteers will develop and choke the opportunities for agency fulfillment.

- *They are flexible.* In a voluntary agency there are frequent changes of schedules and plans, certainly sufficient to discourage anyone. Staff persons may be absolutely ready to accomplish a major task before the end of the week only to find that the responsible volunteer has completely changed the schedule or is unavailable to carry out his or her part of it. The successful staff person has got to be able to adjust and to concentrate on those tasks which are attainable.

- *They have a high amount of patience and tolerance.* Staff persons work with a wide variety of volunteers who are often at their most excitable pitch. The more vibrant and active an agency, the more this will hold true. A staff person has got to be a stable and patient human being or the emotional aspects of working together for significant goals will get out of hand.

- *They are mature.* Psychologists define maturity as the ability to forgo short-term satisfactions in favor of long-term goals. This applies to organizations as well as individuals and particularly does it apply to successful staff persons. Most goals are long range and require persistent, dogged pursuit through all kinds of difficulties. The satisfactions are rarely found on a weekly or even monthly basis. It's only as the agency looks back from a longer perspective that the attainments are visible and the satisfactions present.

- *They're willing to work hard.* Successful people usually work hard, and this is particularly true in the voluntary agency field. There is so very much to be done, the dedication of the volunteers is so high, and the number of forces to be dealt with so great that the only way to achieve success is by working awfully hard.

LOCATING PEOPLE WHO CAN SUCCEED

Committees and staff directors must recognize the size of the recruiting job. Recruitment of the staff head is the most important decision the board will make and selections of staff subordinates are the most important decisions the staff director will make. Despite this, recruitment is too often almost casually approached. As a result, persons who are not really qualified are too often selected.

If the job involves the post of executive director, then a committee should be appointed by the Board of Directors. It is essential that a majority of the committee be composed of board members, but it can also include an able staff person or two from other agencies in the community. If there is a parent organization, a key volunteer or staff person from that group should also serve. The first task of the committee is to decide on the skills and attributes necessary. These will constitute a checklist for later interviewing and should immediately be translated into a job description, salary scale and even into the advertisements if these are to be used.

In terms of salary scales, helpful information is usually available from the health and welfare council, the parent organization or, if necessary, through a quick survey which the chairperson of the committee can do on a confidential basis with the presidents of other, like agencies. Most agencies are willing to cooperate on a volunteer-to-volunteer basis, particularly if they know they will receive a summary of the findings for use in appraising their own salary scales.

When discussing the profiles of people who do and do not succeed in these jobs, I said that most people would not fit the profile of success. This makes it extremely difficult to find those people most likely to succeed. I've found that the simplest way to solve this problem is to locate someone who has already demonstrated a capacity to succeed in this unique milieu. For this reason I constantly, repeatedly and doggedly advise Search Committees and staff directors to look within the agency for experienced or promising people. When I refer to the agency I mean the nationwide group with which you are affiliated. If that doesn't apply in your case, then I advise checking with those directors of major agencies which are in your area. In other words, I would do almost anything to find candidates who have already demonstrated a capacity to succeed in this peculiar kind of work. Having seen the grief and trouble which agencies suffer as a result of hiring the wrong people, I wish I could be sitting across from you now to make this point so positively that you would realize how totally I have learned this lesson.

I am constantly told that it's better to locate a person who knows the local scene. I don't believe it. A bright, effective community organizer is going to see that local scene and develop those contacts in lightning-fast time. Indeed he or she is not encumbered by some of the difficulties which the local resident might have. These difficulties involve the set ways in which individuals are already perceived (as someone's kid sister, being associated with the North Side, having worked for the other newspaper, and so on).

By the time you've developed your list of skills and attributes, you'll be overwhelmed by your findings that the person you need will have to be very mature, very experienced, and brilliantly able. This, in turn, will suggest an older person. But the experience of many agencies, and certainly the experience of the Peace Corps, VISTA, Office of Economic Opportunity, and other groups, makes clear how fast a young, dedicated person can learn and how much this dedication means in achieving success.

For many years I was involved in a trainee program. In that process, we recruited young people who received brief training prior to their first job placement in a volunteer agency setting. These individuals quickly grew to be significant staff leaders and their youth was an asset rather than a liability. This program allowed us to carefully screen people who had the attributes of success, and job experience provided most of the necessary skills. My strong advice to you is to look for the person who is likely to succeed based on fitting the profile rather than finding someone whose age would seem to be an advantage.

You may find you want to do some advertising. This can be done both through newspapers and through organization and professional journals. Use newspaper advertising only when you have not been able to generate enough candidates by close examination of personnel rosters in the organization and by talking to other agency executives. When turning to advertising, deliberately slant the ads to attract persons who have had related experience. Write the ads in such a way that you screen out as many unprepared people as possible; otherwise you will be absolutely inundated with replies.

At times professional employment services are helpful. In addition to government and private employment agencies, professional societies often have employment services of their own. My experience has indicated that you need to be adamant about the kind of people you want and the kind of people you don't want. These agencies, particularly the private ones, want to give their current roster of job seekers a feeling of activity and for that purpose will send all kinds of unqualified candidates. I insist on advance resumés and I *never* accept the employment agency's reference checking as very thorough.

One last word of caution on where to look. Beware of the board member who has a friend. More agencies make bad decisions because the Search Committees find it awkward to decide against the friend of the president or a person pushed hard by a board member. The smaller the community the tougher this is. Board members will feel sorry for a woman newly widowed or a county commissioner unfairly defeated, and the Search Committee will suddenly and totally ignore common sense and/or sound procedures. The result is that the most important decision the board can make ends up by being badly made. This applies, too, to the staff director. He should never give in to any pressure to hire a person who doesn't fit the profile needed. This may seem fairly obvious, but many staff people find themselves deciding in favor of friends of board members because it's awkward to ignore the advice. The goal should be to hire the best possible people, and the thrill and result of doing that will outweigh any short-term awkwardness from turning aside the importunity of anyone.

SCREENING, INTERVIEWING, AND DECIDING

The ideal way to screen candidates is not always available. However, if it is, I urge you to take advantage of it. If you are part of a larger organization, let the parent organization do the initial screening. Be definite with them in terms of the skills and attributes you want and ask them to provide three or four people whom they view as ready for such an assignment.

If you don't have the luxury of a parent organization to do this and do it well, or if you're combining that process with some other searching, your next steps should be as follows:

Screen the resumés down to five to seven people and then have someone take a personal look at each. If these prospects are in other cities, ask your sister organizations to take a look at the candidates or you can involve your board people who may travel. Members of your board may have company counterparts in those cities, and this at least gives you an opportunity to know whether the person seems to hold up to his resumé.

When the group is narrowed down, do some very extensive reference checking. I don't put much stock in listed references, although I do contact them and ask very pointed questions. I put much more stock in my telephone conversations with past supervisors. I've learned the hard way that most references and supervisors want to be helpful to the candidate, if only to be rid of him. Accept that this can be the relationship, and therefore work very hard to get down to the facts. It's helpful to explain the importance of the job and the fact that public money will be expended to support it. On this basis, you can make clear how essential it is to get an honest picture of the candidate's qualifications. Make clear how much you are counting on the supervisor's candor. One of the points which I use is that even if the person is hired, I want to know what skills or attributes will need strengthening. This is not only truthful and helpful, it very often is the key to opening up discussion of possible weaknesses.

I'm often on the other side of these calls and, with very few exceptions, I am constantly appalled at how cursory the review really is. As a consequence, I rarely have to be as candid as I feel I would be if the questioning were sharp. This tells me that most people have made up their minds, but still want to go through the steps of clearance without having their decision shaken. My approach is to shake the daylights out of my judgment. I'd rather face the error at that stage than when the person is on the job. The two things, then, that you have going for you in getting a candid appraisal are the opportunity to make clear how concerned you are about spending public money well and your desire to check the supervisor rather closely on the grounds that even if a favorable decision is made, you want to know what skills and attributes you can help the candidate to better develop.

Some candidates stipulate that no checking be done. They make the good case that they are simply looking into a situation and until they are sure they want to apply, they would rather not stir things up. At times you will have to abide by this. Have it understood, however, that if a person does become a finalist, the checking will have to be done before anything is firmed up. This stage is often skipped. You will have screened the person (except for the reference checking), have interviewed him, and have decided that he or she's the best. There'll be a feeling of euphoria that you've finally located the right person and there's no sense in going through the awkwardness of postponing firming it up when you are so confident that the decision is correct. Resist closure under these circumstances until the reference checking is done. I have learned over the years that the majority of people don't succeed in this field and consequently there are many inefficient people in it, many of whom contradict their low level of general performance by being superior at selling themselves in job interviews.

If you are hiring a staff director, have the full committee see the candidates, if possible, during the span of the same day, or on successive days.

If you're a staff person hiring other staff, it is helpful to ask board members and other staff members to meet the candidate. Don't do this in a group, but give the candidate a chance to know more about you and the agency by talking to other people who work for you and by talking to volunteers who are close enough to the operation to participate in a free give-and-take about the operation and about you.

When a Search Committee is involved, the group should take time to decide how they'll conduct themselves during the interviews. The committee should develop a list of skills and attributes and clear any revisions in the job description and salary scale with the Board of Directors. (It's usually a pretty good idea to check the job description, anyway, because there's no better time to change the job description than when the post is vacant.)

Please, please don't play games during the interviews. I've been involved in situations where members of the committee or the committee as a whole tried to shake up the candidate or tried in other ways to "see what the candidate is really made of." That's a good way of turning off your best candidates. The better way is to approach the interview through straightforward, candid discussion of the job and the candidate. The goal is to objectively determine if there is a match or a potential mismatch between the job description and the candidate. It's useful to describe real-life situations in the organization and to ask the candidate almost as though he were an organization consultant to share initial suggestions for dealing with those situations.

It's important, too, to candidly explain any reservations the committee has about the individual in terms of gaps in experience, possible weak areas, a questionable reference check, and the like. Remember that it's a two-way proposition. Help the candidate to screen himself or herself out. This is hard to do because you want to present a favorable picture. It's human nature to want people to want the job but, on the other hand, it's better to be candid if that helps a candidate recognize that he is just not matched for what you really want. Better to learn it at this stage than later. If the selection process is strung out at all, keep the candidates posted. This is a courtesy too often overlooked. Not doing it can result in some of your good people becoming disenchanted with your lack of thoughtfulness.

Naturally, the committee's own instincts will play a significant part in the final recommendation. It is advisable, however, to introduce some objective measures in order to check your intuition and to be certain that each candidate is being viewed in light of the same criteria. My suggestion to Search Committees is that they take the attributes and skills and set out a kind of score sheet. I usually suggest a rating of 0 to 5, with 5 being the highest mark. It's a good idea not to use these score sheets during the interview, but, instead, to take a few minutes after each interview for the committee members to mark their score cards. This is one of the reasons it is useful to see the candidates on the same day, or on successive days. It brings a little more uniformity into the process.

After you've rated all the candidates, I predict the committee will be surprised at the scores. I don't suggest that the scores will necessarily contradict instinct, but you will be fascinated by the fact that some candidates who just didn't seem very impressive will come up with good scores. This leads to a much more objective discussion of the candidates in relation to the skills and attributes you are really looking for. One individual may not be terribly dramatic but, on scores, comes up pretty solidly right across the board. You may still decide on the individual who has more flair, but, again, you may not. It's the scoring which will lead you to know what you're deciding.

I've never had a chance to do any research on this, but I think I have had experience enough to predict that when this more scientific method is used, the committee will end up hiring someone who would not have been their first choice if left to their own instincts. I would further guess that they would agree then and two years later that their instincts, to some extent, had deceived them.

I follow this process in promoting and hiring, so it's not just something that applies in the Search Committee process. There have been times when I have known for certain who were the right persons for given posts, but still have made myself go through the exercise of trying to objectively identify skills and attributes and to rate the several people. In the end, I have found that my obvious candidates were at least surprisingly well challenged and sometimes overtaken.

Good judgment is based on sound analysis, and sound analysis is based on accurate data.

The Search Committee reports to the Board of Directors. If it is not possible for the full board to be involved in the decision, the Executive Committee would usually have that authority. Some organizations give the

Search Committee final authority to identify one choice and then refer the candidate to the Board of Directors or Executive Committee. I tend to favor the Search Committee's narrowing the field down to two to four people and then having the Executive Committee do the final interviewing. In this case, the Executive Committee should follow the interviewing procedure which was outlined above. This process involves the full Executive Committee, which, in turn, means that the most experienced people in the agency are participating. This also means that the full committee will have some real commitment to the candidate selected.

If both the Search and Executive Committees are to be involved in the interviewing, this can be done in tandem to save time and expense. For example, the Search Committee can see seven people on Friday and refer three to the Executive Committee on Saturday.

If the position involved is not that of staff director, then the choice should be entirely that of the staff person who will be responsible for the supervision. A staff person may want his own superior to interview a candidate just to get another perspective, but the superior should not have a veto right. Similarly, the board members may be asked to help screen and interview applicants for a department head, but the final decision should rest completely with the executive director.

Follow a strict timetable for selecting an executive director. Don't string it out. Prolonged search operations are unhealthy for the organization's morale and are unnecessarily awkward. At the local level the process should not require more than three months, including determining the attributes and skills, developing the job description and salary scale, and the searching and screening.

ARRANGEMENTS AND FOLLOW-UP

The personnel policies and the letter confirming the appointment should indicate that there is a six-month probation period. This should apply to all professional positions. During the probation period, the new staff person should be entitled to the basic fringe benefits. The confirming letter should also cover all the essential understandings, including salary, salary scale, moving costs, starting date, and so on. The candidate should be asked to return a signed copy of the letter for the personnel records.

I am frequently asked if there should be a contract, and I almost always say No. I acknowledge that when I became executive director of the National Association for Mental Health, the management consulting firm which was involved in the search had already written into the procedures that there would be a three-year contract. When that contract expired, however, I made no move to have it renewed. My own feeling is that a board must be free to change executive directors. If a person goes into a situation hopeful of being able to handle it, that's part of the gamble. I know this doesn't add much to job security, but I guess I just don't feel that job security is an available luxury in this business. It's important to acknowledge that many experienced people in the field strongly disagree with me on the matter of contracts, but, as often as I've heard them out, I always come away wondering whether contracts really mean that much.

An important consideration which can't be generalized is the matter of timing of the change. Try to follow the golden rule so that you are not trying to hurry a starting date beyond what you would consider reasonable if you were losing one of your own. I do recommend that people take a good block of time off before starting a new job. This is an important transition with a good deal of emotional and physical stress at both ends. Therefore, if at all possible, there should at least be two months between the agreement and the starting date.

It's usually helpful to have the new staff people make a trip or two to the office before starting. This can involve them in board meetings or other major events so that, even though they are not to start for a while, they begin to get a feel of what is going on. Obviously, too, there can be a good deal of reading about the operation during this period. Note that most voluntary organizations don't try to cover additional expenses such as reimbursement for costs of selling real estate, cost of selling the house, paying differential or mortgage rates, and so on.

Please *do* send letters to the references, prior supervisors and present employers of the person selected. This is a courtesy almost always overlooked, and thus many people are left quite up in the air as to what happened. Particularly, if you are in a public organization, this will help in your own public relations. The president or the chairperson of the Search Committee should personally call the other finalists to thank them for their participation and to outline the final decision. Let the candidates ask questions about the impression they made. This can be useful to them in future situations. Lastly, if the new director is from another city he or she will profit from as much help as you can give in getting settled in and oriented to the new community.

5.
Training and
Holding a Good Staff

During my period of service with the American Heart Association I had the opportunity to serve as chairman of a committee which developed a "Design for Training." This was a manual to assist staff in the orientation, basic training and continuing training of other staff. A considerable portion of what I've included in this chapter grew out of that experience. I've adapted some of the material to apply to agencies in general, and I've supplemented it with a good deal of other experiences and references. I have not tried to identify each credit in my liberal use of AHA's "Design for Training." However, I readily acknowledge how significantly I leaned on that experience and that manual in putting this chapter together.

ORIENTATION

Under an earlier section dealing with orientation of volunteers, I mentioned that most organizations assume that new recruits somehow gain by osmosis a sense of the history of the organization and an awareness of the significant body of knowledge relating to the agency. This applies also to staff persons. Even when an elaborate recruitment program takes place, once the person is hired, the agency breathes a sigh of relief and assumes that somehow the orientation will take place and that, at the very least, the staff person will learn through baptism by fire. That's one way to provide orientation, but it's also a way to discourage and limit the usefulness of the new recruit.

Orientation is the responsibility of the supervisor. In the case of a new executive director, orientation is the president's responsibility. The president might appoint a special small committee to be sure that the basic process of orientation is taking place. If you are part of a large association, the parent group should be put to work.

Orientation takes place during the first three to six months of employment. The general objectives are: (1) to acquaint the new staff person with the office and office procedures; (2) to identify and acquaint the new staff person with the job responsibilities and duties; (3) to provide full information about working relationships with co-workers; (4) to inform and interpret the personnel policies and practices of the association, including working conditions, payroll information, fringe benefits and so on; (5) to provide an introduction to and working relationship with the volunteer leadership of the association; (6) to identify the program goals and objectives of the association and its affiliates; (7) to identify and clarify the job responsibilities and contributions of the different levels of the association which provide for the development of the total program of the agency; (8) to outline the schedule of work; (9) to provide an introduction to the training program, including conditioning to criticism; (10) to interpret the role of the agency in the community; and (11) to give an overview and initial presentation of the major activities of the association.

The methods and techniques used are as follows: (1) planned conferences; (2) informal discussions of brief duration to answer an immediate problem or to offer assurance; (3) sessions and work experiences arranged with other staff members; (4) review and study of files and minutes; (5) attendance at committee and staff meetings; (6) visits to other agencies; (7) visits to other affiliates of the same agency; (8) review of association pamphlets and films; (9) reading assignments; and (10) interviews with selected volunteer leaders, including committee chairpersons.

Though the subjects to be covered are fairly obvious I've found it useful to keep a listing handy. In case my listing will be helpful to you, these are the basic points of information:

> *History of the association*
> *The cause itself*
> *Basic mission of the organization*
> *How we serve*
> *Examples of program*
> *Relative roles of volunteers and staff*
> *Current priorities and projects*
> *Who does what*
> *Policies and position statements*
> *Finances*
> *The community*
> *Our major assets and major problems*
> *My ground rules for staff operations and performance*

DEFINING SKILLS

Just some of the demands made on a general staff member in a voluntary agency are:

1. Know the community and the resources that are available.
2. Effectively apply community organization principles and techniques.
3. Ability to express one's self both orally and in writing.
4. Understanding of the committee process plus ability to serve as staff representative to committees.
5. Able to assume responsibility for sophisticated program administration.
6. Ability to analyze fund-raising operations.
7. Ability to direct a fund-raising campaign.
8. Thorough grounding in budgeting, cost analysis, and financial reporting.
9. Skill in working with radio, TV and newspapers.
10. Able to write annual reports, newsletters, and committee reports.
11. Demonstrated efficiency in office management and job organization.
12. Effectiveness in staff recruitment, orientation and training.
13. Experience with interpersonal relationships, thus qualifying the staff person to work effectively with hundreds of volunteers who have various interests and motivations.

Many, if not most, of the persons now performing the job described above have not had prior voluntary agency experience. Indeed, prior to employment in their current jobs, they had little knowledge or experience in most of the above tasks. Generally, speaking when the skills required are matched against the background of most of the job-holders, the chasm is gigantic. This situation becomes all the more pressing when the significant missions of these voluntary organizations are studied, and one realizes the tremendous public responsibility which is involved. Because of budget problems and unrealistic aspirations, most agencies simply throw their staff people into the breach, hoping that learning by doing will somehow fill the bill.

STAFF DEVELOPMENT

A president or staff person who accepts responsibility for supervising others, accepts responsibility for helping those persons grow. Voluntary agencies, in general, have neglected their staff development responsibility. There are some exciting exceptions—for instance, the programs of both the Boy Scouts and Girl Scouts—but generally staff persons are not provided opportunities to achieve a match of skills and expectations.

Supervisors too often equate *training* with *orientation.* Actually, however, the process is much more involved. Training itself is primarily the result of on-the-job experience with supervision. Most people assume that training involves mainly reading, briefings, and/or special courses, when in fact real training is practising under close supervision and practising with general consultation.

Whether it be a one-person staff or a larger operation, these are the basic steps for effective training:

1. Create an open work-situation which will encourage exchange of ideas.
2. Encourage the learning situation by providing staff with opportunities to perform assignments that challenge their abilities.
3. Stimulate staff to higher achievements by maintaining standards of performance.
4. Establish and utilize a performance rating system

that periodically acquaints each staff member with his or her progress.

5. Provide effective supervision, including individual counseling if necessary.
6. Make group training experiences available to staff.
7. Provide subordinates with full opportunity to participate in goal-setting for themselves and the agency.
8. Pay realistic attention to these motivational factors which are of the greatest concern to those participating:
   —gaining group approval and respect,
   —desiring to succeed on the new job,
   —desiring to grow on the job,
   —financial return.

Even this minimal process may seem well beyond the limits of time a president can devote to it, but it still can be planned for. In almost any community there are personnel specialists, effective agency experts and others, who will agree to serve on a Personnel Committee which includes staff development as its core responsibility. Both the president and staff person in a one-person office may initially resist taking time for this purpose, but it's at this level that staff development is usually most needed and most neglected. It has been my experience that in short order both the president and executive director will delight in the benefits from such an arrangement.

Many state and national voluntary organizations try, like businesses, to provide a complete pattern of training courses so that an individual will have an opportunity to be formally trained for the skills required. This begins with a delineation of the needed skills, an appraisal, usually done by somebody up above in the organization, of the upgrading necessary to achieve those skills, and a planned schedule of training courses.

These programs usually involve training courses put on by the parent organization, supplemented by local orientation and refresher courses. They are, of course, dependent on an effective process of supervision including goal setting and evaluation.

Some organizations, through budget stringencies or enlightened new approaches, have undertaken self-development plans. These, too, begin with an appraisal of performance standards and tasks, but then lead into greater *self*-appraisal of improvement needed and *self*-direction in seeking assistance to develop necessary skills. Individuals involved in such a program are usually assisted by a staff development specialist in their self-assessment of unmet standards and in the development of their learning plans.

Many agencies are combining these two models. This grows out of both budget limitations and an awareness that if individuals are really to grow, they must be intimately involved in determining their own development plans.

A few years ago I was involved in a project designed to meet some emergency training needs. The California Heart Association was at a stage where the organization was developing far more rapidly than we could realistically handle. We faced a tremendous need to quickly develop new staff skills. We worked with the local staff members throughout the state in identifying the skills they felt most in need of. Then we worked together to develop a profile which identified the skills the person's job required and a mutual determination of which of those skills most needed developing. We then identified the formal courses which were available within the American Heart Association and, where appropriate, targeted people for these.

We developed certain other courses which the California affiliate was trained to conduct. Other courses needed to be developed on an interagency basis, and we developed these in conjunction with the American Lung Association, the National Society for Crippled Children and Adults, and the American Cancer Society. Lastly, we identified the relevant continuing education courses offered by educational institutions within California. Through this process we were able to identify or develop the resources to deal with most of the skills needed and to project a training schedule for each professional staff member.

During that same California crisis we also developed a trainee program which attracted to the Association younger people who wanted a career in public service. We did not try to hire students right out of college or graduate school for the trainee program because the first jobs into which most of these people would be placed required that they have work experience. Therefore, we turned to persons who had been involved in other activities for one to five years and who were looking for a change into something such as we were offering.

We provided one month of training in the state office, four months of placement in a local chapter, and a final one-month wrap-up again at the state office. Most of these people were quickly moved into jobs throughout the state and have since developed into significant staff leaders within the Heart Association and other agencies.

A new development which is hopeful and will bear watching is the United Way's newly formed National Academy for Voluntarism. It can be an important supplement to training for both staff and volunteers of agencies affiliated with United Way. The academy will include a facility at the University of Miami but, more importantly, will involve outreach extension courses throughout the country so that many agencies can regularly participate in a series of courses thoughtfully developed to meet the needs of voluntary agencies.

KEEPING THEM

Earlier in this chapter I gave an indication of the skills and attributes necessary for a staff person if he or she is really going to be able to do the job well. Given this unique profile and the breadth of activities encompassed, staff turnover is a very costly business. Yet most voluntary agencies still do not approach the important business of retaining good people with anything like the priority it deserves.

Holding onto good staff is not wholly, nor even largely, a matter of salary and benefits. These people want a sense of purpose, contribution and fulfillment. In 1959 Frederick Herzberg published his research under the title of *The Motivation to Work* which established that achievement, recognition, work itself, responsibility and advancement are the primary sources of job satisfaction. This is particularly true of the kind of person who tackles the staff role in a voluntary agency. It is essential that there be some regular pattern of training opportunities for refreshment and self-renewal. These jobs grind a person down and unless there is a means by which a person can be restored and refreshed, the zeal and patience are whittled away.

Certainly one can't dismiss the importance of realistic salary scales and fringe benefits. These must be a part of the effort to attract, promote and hold good people. Fringe benefits should include basic medical, major medical and retirement coverage, and the program should be transferred automatically if a person moves within a state or national organization. The salary scale should be competitive with other agencies at a level realistic enough that the person is not constantly torn by his failure to provide basic needs for his family.

Throughout this book I've talked about the importance of volunteers and the essentially subordinate role of staff, but none of that is to deny the importance of good staff in a large voluntary agency. It's tragic the way most agencies chew up good people and then wonder why the organization isn't lunging forward. Far more of the voluntary organization's planning and resources should go into building and nurturing a career development effort.

6.
Constructive Planning

A pretty good description of planning in voluntary organizations could be summarized as "we'll do as much good as we possibly can and that's all we can do." There is somehow an assumption that, because the mission is so large and the purposes so desperately important, it is not possible, nor perhaps even humane, to try to define what is most important if this means conscientiously deciding that certain important goals may not be reached.

BRIGHT IDEAS AND UNREALISTIC HOPES

One of the principal results of trying to accomplish more than is attainable is that all accountability is lost. It's not possible to expect or require someone to be finished with a task by next Friday or April 30, if the individual can automatically come back and say that he or she is so swamped with other assigned tasks that there is just no way that this new task can be done. Presidents and executive directors of voluntary organizations start out each year with such sweeping expectations that as the months pass and it becomes obvious that most of these expectations can't be fulfilled there is a tendency to get discouraged and to begin to hope that next year might be different.

In the absence of more realistic planning, most voluntary agencies are governed, and badly so, by the *bright idea.* A president, committee chairperson, board member or staff member gets a bright idea about what should be done and off the agency zags. The organization is almost defenseless against the bright idea because it sounds so good or might help so many people, for there is no mechanism to put it in competition with all the other things that might be done. The board, in particular, is frustrated because most of the board members aren't close enough to really know what's going on and they can't quite grasp just where the agency is and why. They are also confused because there seems almost no way to evaluate what is already being done.

What planning is taking place is probably related only to what staff thinks the agency should be doing. This is another example of the way agency control drifts (or is pulled) in the direction of staff dominance. Many thoughtful volunteers have concluded that planning is always going to be a staff role because only staff have the kind of continuity, overview, and the time to plan. I don't agree. Indeed, I think if volunteers can't be put in charge of planning, voluntaryism is considerably weakened.

One of the problems of effective volunteer involvement in planning is that people, particularly planners, always make planning seem so complicated. I've consulted with planning officers of large corporations in trying to improve my own approach to planning, only to be put off with the jargon and makework of what to me is an unnecessarily complicated process. It doesn't need to be so overwhelming.

PLANNING FOR THE YEAR AHEAD

It is entirely realistic to engage in an intelligent approach to planning without having the process engulf all available time. For several years I've participated in an annual "Planning Retreat" designed to give the organization's officers an opportunity to effectively decide where they want to be a year hence. I've used this process at the local, state and national levels, and in all cases have found it to have tremendous benefits. The process of an annual Planning Retreat begins with the president asking board members, committee chairpersons, staff members, and others what they consider to be the most important tasks to accomplish in the current year. These are carefully cataloged for advance study by the officers. The agency's top volunteer and staff leaders then go into a two-day concentrated planning session which is designed to identify but not to undertake the major projects and goals for the year and to determine to whom they will be assigned. The object of the Planning Retreat is to develop what I call the Annual Agenda for the year. The Annual Agenda is the organization's carefully-planned objectives for the year ahead. If the agency has had an opportunity to develop its five-year goals, the Annual Agenda should, of course, relate closely to these.

A typical agenda for an officers' Planning Retreat should, then, include these topics:

Review of our mission.
Review of our current resources.

What did we get done in the past twelve months?
What didn't we get done?
Review of our continuing responsibilities.
What *has* to be done in the next twelve months?
Can we get it done?
What's it going to take?
What important projects can't we do next year?
Can we get the board to agree?
Who's going to be responsible for what?

If yours is a typical group, this process will represent the first time your leadership group will have gained a common perception of what's most important to do *and* what can't be done.

As a starter, it will be revealing and useful to have each individual privately list the two or three things he or she considers most important to accomplish in the year ahead. While these are being recorded and tabulated, ask the group to list the assets or strengths of the association and also the liabilities or problems. I can almost guarantee that these simple approaches will set the stage for some very solid planning. The group, as a group, will begin to have a common grasp of where the organization stands and an appreciation of the diverse and impossible expectations of its leaders. This should quickly lead to the heart of the session which is to decide what is *in fact* possible and what is *really* most important.

The process of an annual Planning Retreat has benefits far beyond even the significant advantage of giving a clear idea of where you're going. For instance, the very nature of the session provides the officers with a common grasp of existing commitments and resources. Also, by being involved in the planning, the officers feel a commitment to the goals for the year. These factors increase their capacity for teamwork and reduce the many frictions and break-downs in communication which could later occur.

One of the most exciting aspects of these Planning Retreats is the camaraderie which develops. We sometimes forget that the volunteer officers, even if they live in the same neighborhood or city, often don't know one another very well, and frequently have quite different perceptions of the organization. By battling out the difficult decisions about how to utilize limited resources, the individuals really come together as a group. It's important to note that the Planning Retreats are not easy sessions. Properly organized, they should be designed to decide what *not* to attempt to accomplish, or what should be assigned low priority, and this obviously means that some of the individuals will be disappointed. However, through more than fifteen years of this process at the local, state and national levels, I have never known a case where the end result was not a tightly knit and enthusiastic team.

Still another advantage of the Planning Retreat is that the individuals in the organization come out of the session and the subsequent board meeting on the offensive—that is, they know where they want to go and they're determined to get there.

One of the real advantages of the resulting Annual Agenda is that it provides the officers and staff with an ability to say No to all the pressing, vital bright ideas which come along during the year. These are the things that put an organization on a zigzag course. If an idea or project obviously needs to be dealt with, at least the officers and board can make a conscientious decision about it when they know that this has to compete with their carefully determined goals. It's always amazing that even after going through this involved process, one of the tough jobs of the organization is to stay on course. If an association is dealing with a critical public problem, there will be many calls for a reappraisal of decisions and many new proposals for priority effort, but at least the process of the Planning Retreat and the existence of the Annual Agenda provide ammunition for holding the line.

Many voluntary agencies have had experience in the planning process in the fund-raising area. If an agency says it's going to raise 25 per cent more money, it has to be very specific about the sources and the work plan to achieve it or the results are bound to be very disappointing.

The existence of an Annual Agenda makes the whole organization more aware of the need to accomplish the most important tasks. There should be reports to the Executive Committee and Board of Directors involving the volunteer leaders responsible for each of the areas of activity, and everyone should know that the progress is being charted.

It's a good idea to print your Annual Agenda on large posters to be available at board meetings. If your board and committees generally meet in one place, affix a set of these posters on the wall and, if possible, show the degree of fulfillment to date. These devices may sound terribly managerial and, indeed, are foreign to voluntary agencies, but unless citizen groups learn to identify the most important things to be done and then find ways to lock in resources to accomplish them, we will continue to be characterized as inefficient do-gooders.

There are, of course, still more sophisticated levels of planning, involving such things as quantification of goals, but my experience has been that the planners usually scare voluntary agencies away from sensible beginnings by making planning sound more involved than it really needs to be. Along the same line, a word of caution about the involvement of professional planners. Obviously it's wise to take advantage of solid experience in any specialty, including planning. However, carefully select someone who knows your organization and who is realistic. Most planners want to immediately bring the organization to a level of sophistication far beyond the time or resources that can be realistically assigned.

FUTURE GOALS

Most of what I've described above represents an effort on the part of the current officers to gain a grasp of where they want to be at the end of their terms and to have some means of locking in resources to get there. Several times, however, I've referred to the relationship of this process to the five-year goals of the agency. Here, too, I don't want to scare people off with the complexities of a process, but obviously an agency dealing with a longer-term effort should have an idea where it wants to go in the next five years. This process, too, should involve and emphasize volunteer participation. It doesn't really have to be so terribly complicated; indeed, most things come down to common sense and some rudimentary skills. In the area of five-year planning, a volunteer group should be assigned to take a careful look at the mission of the organization, the current goals, the progress toward those goals, and the available resources. This, in turn, will begin to help the board think about what is most important to be done six and seven years hence. A good deal of time should be allowed for the process so that there can be plenty of give-and-take about what the various elements of the organization believe are important. This process may develop some intense debates and perhaps cause some people to go away upset, but, in the end, the membership and board will have had an opportunity to think through where they've been, where they are, and where they're going, along with what they consider to be the most promising steps for moving closer to the fulfillment of the agency's mission.

Keep in mind the Peter Principle "if you don't know where you're going, you'll end up someplace else." I would add to this that, in a voluntary agency, if you don't know where you're going, you'll end up zigging and zagging in all directions. *But* if the volunteers have been involved in a common-sense approach to figuring out what the resources are and how best to assign them, you're more likely to end up with a giant step in the direction of the organization's basic purpose.

7.
The Membership, Board of Directors, and Committees

Management specialists are increasingly inclined to suggest that the number to be involved in a decision should be determined according to *the principle of least number.* For practical purposes, they suggest, one ought constantly to narrow down to the fewest possible people those who will be involved in a decision or activity. These management specialists have absolutely given up on me, for in the voluntary setting I believe that authority should be moved toward the largest number capable of exercising it. If an organization is dealing with a major public problem, maximum participation in defining the problem and its solution represents the shortest route to community action. A complaint one can anticipate from businessmen newly elected to a board is that far too many people serve on the board and its committees.

A few people making decisions for the whole organization is efficient if it's a business-type organization. However, if those decisions are going to have to be sold to those who will be affected in the community or in other parts of the organization—and if there is no strong legislative or line authority for requiring compliance—then even these businessmen begin to learn that the shortest route to making the right decisions and having them carried out is via *a process of maximum feasible involvement.*

VOTING MEMBERSHIP

It will come as no surprise that I believe the Voting Membership of an organization should have a far larger role and greater authority than is usually the case. People are easily and naturally confused about the definition of "Voting Members." Most Certificates of Incorporation identify some body beyond the Board of Directors as having ultimate authority. The usual characterization of this group is "Voting Membership." Voting Members are those responsible for convening once a year to elect the Board of Directors. In many agencies there is considerable confusion as to who is a Voting Member, with the result that the Board of Directors usually functions in this role or, at the other extreme, all contributors are considered as Voting Members.

Have a Voting Membership at least four times the size of the Board of Directors. The group should be as large as possible so long as individuals actually accept election as Voting Members with the knowledge that this carries at least some nominal responsibility. A Voting Membership can be quickly built from the rosters of the current board, past board members, current committee members, past committee members, current larger contributors, professionals interested in the association's work, representation from the various neighborhoods or geographic areas served by the organization, constituents who have been assisted by the agency, and selected representatives of groups the association wants to cultivate, such as news media, the chamber of commerce, various minority groups, local schools, other agencies, and public officials. Voting Members should be officially advised of their selection with an opportunity to accept or reject. The responsibilities are not burdening, but they should be willing to receive and read reports from the organization, attend the Annual Meeting, and be available to consider committee assignments and volunteer opportunities.

There are obvious advantages in having a large number of persons who are sufficiently interested to accept Voting Membership status. The program of the organization, whatever it may be, is bound to be helped if only by broader awareness of who can be helped, what is needed, and public understanding. Clearly the public image of the organization will grow along with the quality and quantity of persons attached to it. The fund-raising implications are clear. And there is a growing pool of potential volunteers for special assignments and for future election to the Board of Directors of the organization. Keeping this group informed represents a responsibility and also a stunning opportunity. We too often want to tell our story directly to the public, forgetting that a growing cadre of Voting Members is a solid means of spreading the word.

The Annual Membership Meeting should absorb much of your attention in order to stimulate maximum attendance, knowledgeable discussion, and a growing respect for the accomplishments and plans of the organization. While it will take time, I favor moving as rapidly as possible in the direction of submitting major decisions to the Voting Membership. Initially this might be done to gain their reaction to issues, but eventually I hope it would be for decisions. These would include changes in the bylaws, election of officers, approval of five-year plans, and other major matters relating to significant changes in the association's directions and operations. It is also important that the board meetings be open ones with prior notice to all Voting Members, including an indication of the subjects to be covered and decisions that will be recommended.

I know these proposals will dismay most executive directors, presidents and board members, but I am convinced that if a voluntary agency is to truly reach out to deal effectively with broad public problems, there must be this kind of involvement and careful cultivation of maximum community participation.

BOARD OF DIRECTORS

The board members should represent those individuals who, in the significant majority, have proven their interest in the cause and their ability to help pursue it. Chairpersons and members of committees should be the first logical source. The Voting Membership should represent a basic pool for new board members. There will be times when the Nominating Committee will recognize a particular need which is not yet matched by persons serving anywhere in the organization and, in such cases, board members might be selected from the community at large. I regularly urge Nominating Committees to look first and foremost within the organization. There is too great a tendency to overleap the people who have proven themselves in hopes of getting bigger names or greater influence. My experience has been that the way you build impact is to build with the people who have proven their interest.

Most organizations regularly question whether their boards are not too large and many organizations are now streamlining their operations so that the boards are relatively small. I feel that a board has to be fairly large if it is to effectively represent the various interests, geographic areas, major association pursuits, minorities, youth, some past leadership, and reasonable participation of new blood. I don't believe there is need to be concerned about larger boards. The counter-argument is that we can't expect all of these people to really have an interest in, or a grasp of, all the things the agency is doing. My experience has been that voluntary agency boards of any size rarely comprise individuals who have across-the-board interest or knowledge. I've found that if a board is effectively organized, there will be people participating who have an intense interest in certain topics, and there will be others who have a like interest in other topics, and that in toto the group will add up to an effective screen for the issues and for reasonable discussion of them. A small board is much more manageable in all ways except in the essential way of achieving follow-through among the multiple constituencies which have to be reached by a broad-based agency dealing with a significant public problem.

The usual solution to managing a large board is to have it meet only rarely and to depend primarily on a small Executive Committee. In my opinion, this is a mistake. Instead, the board should meet frequently and each meeting should be of sufficient duration so that the board can in fact deal with the major decisions of the organization. At the community level I believe a board should meet eight or nine times during the year, and it will need at least three hours for each meeting to get caught up on things, to have a feeling of "being in the know" about exciting new developments in the over-all field, and to tackle the issues at hand. Board members should be used on committees and task forces, with as much spread of responsibility as possible, so that each board member develops a feeling of participation, commitment and understanding.

Persons who cannot be active should be dropped. My approach to this is to provide a clause in the bylaws which automatically drops persons who have missed a certain number of consecutive meetings unless the board officially votes forgiveness. Letters should go annually to those board members whose attendance and participation has been irregular, indicating that in the coming year, the officers will be depending more than ever on them for active participation. If the individual board members feel that this active participation is just not possible within the immediate future because of their schedule, they may choose to change their status to Voting Member.

Board terms should be limited. Generally speaking, a three-year term with a chance for one additional term seems to make sense. After a year off the board, a person can come back on. This recycling should be done with great caution. There is a great temptation on the part of staff and Nominating Committee to yearn for the good old days and past personal associations, but the real emphasis should be on seeking new blood.

An informal listing of the qualifications of the ideal board member has endured for the past thirty or forty years. It's attributed to Michael Davis of the Rosenwald Fund. Here are five of the best:

- Know why the organization exists, and annually review why it should.

- Give money, or help get it, or both.

- Face budgets with courage, endowments with doubt, deficits without dismay, and recover quickly from a surplus.

- Interpret health work to the public in words of two syllables.

- Combine a New England sense of obligation with an Irish sense of humor.

EXECUTIVE COMMITTEE

There is usually a very real need to have an Executive Committee which can act between meetings of the Board of Directors. It's important that the Executive Committee be able to exercise all the powers of the board except changes in the bylaws. This opens the danger of the Executive Committee functioning in place of the Board of Directors, but practicalities necessitate that risk. As a matter of fact, Executive Committees are too often used in place of boards.

The Executive Committee should be large enough to be representative of the Board of Directors. It should not be simply the officers and one or two others. If the Board of Directors is made up of fifty or more people, the Executive Committee should have at least fifteen members. Some Executive Committees include the officers and committee chairpersons. I advise against this, as it puts together a group too easily given to pork barreling and not equipped to give objective review of the emergency matters which will be coming before it.

Executive Committee minutes should be quickly circulated to all board members, and each board meeting should include a report of Executive Committee actions.

OTHER COMMITTEES

In the matter of the number of committees, I agree here with the principle of least number. The Executive

Committee and Board of Directors should handle as many matters as possible. The work of many committees, including the Personnel and Bylaws Committees, can usually be accommodated by ad-hoc assignments as needed. I am a great believer in "ad-hocracy." All committees except those absolutely required and identified in the bylaws should be ad hoc, including the stipulation that they automatically go out of business at the end of the year unless specifically reconstituted and recharged by the board. I am also a great user of "one-person" task forces, or at least "few-person" task forces, which are asked to do their business in one or two meetings and then to automatically go out of business.

If a committee or task force is needed, then look carefully to be certain that the group includes ample representation from the various forces and interests within the organization. In other words, if a committee is really necessary, then make certain that it's large enough to be truly representative of those parts of the community or association concerned with the topic at hand.

Except for the Nominating Committee, the president should have full authority to appoint chairpersons and committees. I don't believe in staggered terms, at least as stipulated by policy or bylaw. This restricts the opportunity of a president to make significant changes when they're needed. The president, instead, should informally stagger the appointments in order to achieve a balance of experience and new blood.

Presidents and boards should not underestimate how much staff time goes into effective service of task forces and committees. Boards, Executive Committees and other committees tend to find that an easy way to deal with conflict is to refer the matter to a new committee. I regularly ask boards whether or not they are doing this because they really want the matter handled by the committee, or whether it's a way to avoid coming to grips with the situation. Board meetings and Annual Meetings should provide an arena for reasonable conflict and resolution of differences. It's better to have a matter done with if this is really the intent rather than prolonging the process just to be polite or to avert conflict. If people knew how very much work is entailed in establishing and servicing such unnecessary appendages, or if they recognized that it cuts into the time available to pursue real priorities, I'm sure a more hardheaded and sensible approach would prevail.

The board should be careful to see that committee activity, to the total extent possible, is pointed toward the program priorities of the organization. It's terribly easy to get caught up in organizational business. For instance, Bylaws Committees often take up more time than any other committee. Everyone is interested in bylaws, even when it's difficult to get those same people moving on priority fund raising and program matters. In the matter of committees, then, I invoke the apt phrase: "Keep your eye upon the doughnut and not upon the hole."

NATIONAL LEVEL CONSIDERATIONS

While most of the comments I've made about the Voting Membership, Board of Directors, Executive Committee, and other committees apply to all levels of an organization, there are additional considerations which apply in the national arena.

The Voting Membership at the national level, for instance, takes on even greater significance and consequently should have an even greater role than the Voting Membership at the community level. For one thing, the constituency will be much more experienced and interested. The

Voting Membership at the national level usually comes from representatives of the constituent local groups. I firmly believe that to the extent possible, the Voting Membership should have an opportunity to advise and make decisions on all major policies and directions. Within the National Association for Mental Health, for instance, the Voting Members have final authority on matters governing:

—standards of affiliation,
—financial relationships policies,
—financial relationships authorization levels,
—bylaw amendments,
—amendments to the certificate of incorporation,
—size of the Board of Directors,
—election of the Board of Directors,
—election and removal of officers.

Resolutions on other matters adopted by the members are subject to the concurrence of the Board of Directors. However, if the board does not concur with a resolution and the Voting Membership passes the resolution a second time, the Voting Membership thereby overrules the board. It is essential that the Voting Membership be proportionately representative, including, if appropriate, some weighting according to financial support.

The Annual Meeting should be seen as a major opportunity for discussion, debate and revitalization. The Voting Members must know that their vote really counts, or they will not take the session seriously, either in terms of attendance or preparation.

A national Board of Directors almost has to be large, and the cost of this, plus the travel involved, will create a considerable temptation to overuse the Executive Committee. I am inclined to feel that 100 members is about the maximum. Beyond that, participation just isn't significant enough to create a feeling of honor and responsibility. It's hard to get much below the number of 100 national board members, however, particularly if there is to be effective representation of all the many groups, forces, and program interests which are so important to national decision-making. If the board is to remain at 100 members or less, it's hard to achieve proportional representation. However, to the extent possible, population should be given weighting.

Committees at the national level are often made up of the individuals who have shown the greatest interest in the subject at hand. This does have a drawback. The people who are the leaders tend to develop even more sophisticated proposals. This is useful, but it tends to leave the majority in the association farther behind. For this reason I tend to give national committees a training responsibility. A committee is responsible for developing new directions, but it is also responsible for making sure that the field is using the guidelines and directions already at hand. This helps, also, to utilize the volunteer talent of the organization to assist in the development of other units.

• Remember that even if your organization has effectively identified the relative roles of the Voting Membership, Board of Directors, Executive Committee and other committees, the success of these various groups will depend almost entirely on the quality of their meetings.

8.
Making the Most Out of Meetings

A significant part of the business of citizens' organizations involves meetings and yet, in most organizations, surprisingly little thought is applied to making these meetings productive. It is a fact of life that good meetings create high attendance, improve the quality of decisions, and promote alert follow-through. Bad meetings do not. Thoughtfulness and common sense are the basic ingredients of planning for good meetings. This, in turn, leads to some rules which make up the art of having good meetings.

BASIC RULES

Give careful attention to the selection, recruitment and orientation of the group, for these are the cornerstones of good meetings. Let me repeat my earlier advice to the presidents that it is important to select as the chairperson an individual who is an effective organizer rather than a person who is an authority on the subject at hand.

The group should have a sense of purpose. Some of this will come with orientation, but it should also be conveyed through the formal committee charge and in the reports from the president, chairperson and others.

Spread the workload of the committee and of the meetings themselves. Try to be certain that several people have responsibility for handling individual items on the agenda.

Always have something that really needs the group's consideration. If you don't, and even though the committee may never have missed a monthly meeting in 133 years, cancel the meeting.

Provide adequate notice and give a reminder call a day or two in advance of the meeting. If it's an ongoing body, have fixed meeting dates such as the first Monday evening of the month. If that's not possible, then it's generally helpful to have the group set its next meeting date while they are still in session. It's important to be certain that the day after the meeting a notice is sent reminding the full group of the next date or dates. It's helpful to put in a return postal card so that you can quickly have an indication of attendance and so that the members make a firm commitment.

Submit the agenda and the basic background material to the full group at least a week in advance of the meeting. I am constantly dismayed when I go to meetings to find how often the agenda is distributed at the meeting, and even then the agenda often consists of three or four nondescript items such as President's Report, Executive's Report, New Business and so on. If the members are worth involving, it's essential that they be served well. The greatest single factor in poor attendance is the failure of the chairperson to provide a good agenda and reference materials well in advance of the meeting. The agenda should clearly state what the group is being asked to consider or decide, and the reference material should prepare the members for intelligent discussion. If the people are committed to attend and if they see that the session is being organized in a businesslike way, they're more likely to be there and at future meetings.

Pay careful attention to the physical arrangements, including the location, accessibility, parking, and reasonable meal service. The room itself should be conducive to effective work, including such basic things as lighting, heat and ventilation. I make an awfully big thing of the way the table is organized. If it's a committee meeting, I try to have a round table or a "square doughnut" so that all the members are facing the center. I find this creates maximum participation and a feeling of involvement for all. Even when I'm dealing with a board meeting of approximately 100 people, I try to organize it in two four-sided or three-sided tiers so that the group is fairly close together, all within earshot of one another, and all facing the center. Even with very large groups, I work hard at trying to create a physical arrangement which is both comfortable and promotes maximum possible involvement. It's essential to plan in advance for blackboards, easels and audio-visual equipment. Be sure to check on electrical outlets, microphones for public address systems and so on. Also don't forget the arrangements for water, coffee service and the like.

Check the meeting room well in advance. It's important the day before the meeting to be certain someone has the work order and that they know you are coming and know what the arrangements are to be. Then I make it a cardinal rule to check the meeting room one hour in advance of the meeting. I do this even with breakfast meetings. My experience is that 50 per cent of the time there is a breakdown in the arrangements. The blackboard will be there, but no chalk. There won't be an extension cord for the projector or the electrical socket will be wired with the lights so that when the lights go out the projector also goes out. Or the public address system won't work or perhaps someone forgot to provide a microphone. And it happens at least 10 per cent of the time that the meeting room isn't set up at all and the only person around never heard of you or your damned meeting. If your meeting is in a hotel, by all means check the bulletin board to be sure the meeting time and place are clearly identified. I'll make a private bet with you that at least 50 per cent of the time the bell captain or the catering department will have listed the wrong meeting room or the wrong time, and that at least 25 per cent of the time they will have forgotten to list you at all. It is always a mystery and frustration to me that hotels which make so much of their money from meetings generally handle them so inadequately and poorly. This is why it's absolutely essential to doggedly check through the arrangements a day in advance and in person an hour in advance.

Abide by Murphy's Laws. There are two laws developed by someone named Murphy who must have learned the hard way, but who left a rich legacy in these cardinal rules for meeting planners:

What can go wrong will go wrong.
If unattended to, it will only get worse.

CONDUCTING A MEETING

Don't let the chairperson or staff member dominate the meeting. If either or both dominate, they may feel terribly good at the end of the session, but they'll be talking to themselves at the next meeting.

Keep the group informed between meetings. This includes getting the minutes out quickly, reporting to the committee on action taken on their recommendations by the Executive Committee or Board of Directors, and thoughtful notes from the chairperson or staff person between meetings, sharing some interesting bits of information or news of the organization's activities. Whatever it is, a deliberate, thoughtful, ongoing effort to let the members know that they are important and are appreciated will pay off.

Give the group a sense of accomplishment and momentum. The original charge to the group should have been realistic enough so that there can be a regular sense of accomplishment. Even if large tasks are broken down into bite sizes, the group can still have a feeling of getting somewhere. Be sure the members do gain a sense of movement and have the satisfaction of accomplishment. Committees and boards often suffer from a feeling of vagueness or vastness, and it takes considerable effort to provide the members with some feeling of tasks well done.

Keep it interesting. Deliberately plan part of the agenda for the purpose of giving the group a feeling of being in the know, having a chance to learn some of the exciting things that are happening in the field, or to know more about what the organization as a whole is doing. I learned a lot from a president who insisted that every meeting should include a section which he labeled "the dancing girls." While it never became quite that interesting, it was his deliberate and successful policy that every meeting should include a film or speaker or some presentation that took the group away from the immediate tasks and gave them a sense of excitement and being in the know.

Pay attention to the niceties. I said in the beginning that these rules grow out of common sense and thoughtfulness. Take time to figure out how to make your meetings pleasant. For instance, people say how much they appreciate having large name placards for each person attending the meeting. These are placed in front of the people and everyone quickly knows or is reminded of everyone else's name. Incidentally, these don't have to be expensive. You can make them out of cutdown manila file folders and let people write their own names with a felt-tip pen. Send the committee list with each agenda. This may seem like duplication, but people do forget names and like to review the list in advance. Include nicknames and women's first names.

Occasionally hold your meeting in a special setting. This doesn't mean it has to be in a fancy club. It might be in one of the facilities which relate to the group's efforts. The National Association for Mental Health encourages local boards to meet at least once a year in the state hospital serving the community.

Provide a regular mechanism for board acknowledgment of committee progress. This kind of thoughtfulness makes a big difference to committee members, who inevitably wonder if their efforts are really noticed and really do achieve results. Thank a committee when its work is done or express appreciation to those who are going off the committee. It's hard to anticipate all the things that add up to the niceties and to thoughtfulness; but, unless presidents, committee chairpersons and staff members take time to project themselves into the place of the members, the rush of everyday events will continue to preoccupy you, and important opportunities to develop a closer feeling of camaraderie and family will be lost.

BOARD MEETINGS ARE SPECIAL

All the basic rules apply in spades to board meetings. In addition, there are special considerations.

The Board of Directors has to have an overview of the mission, goals, progress and problems of the agency, which means that a realistic part of board meetings has to be given over to this kind of review. It can be partly accomplished by a *written* report of the president, including a report of progress toward the Annual Agenda (the one-year plan).

One of the basic and most important roles of the board is to establish the priorities and directions for the organization. This means that realistic time must also be given to discussion and, when appropriate, to approval of the Annual Agenda, the annual budget, and the five-year plan.

The board meeting should begin with, or at least should include, an executive session so that if there are concerns about the executive director's performance, these can be frankly reviewed. The executive session should not be used to review agency operations which should be covered with the executive director present. If the board meets monthly, the executive sessions might be scheduled quarterly. This does not take the place of the annual evaluation of the executive director's performance by the Board of Directors or the Executive Committee.

Because the board's decisions are so central to an agency's effectiveness, it is all the more necessary that the agenda and related material go out in advance. The board members should have an agenda in their hands at least a week in advance of the meeting. The supporting material should not be so voluminous that it will not be practical for board members to gain a grasp of the issues. This means that a good deal of work will have to be done by the president and executive director in order to reduce complicated issues down to their essence. Some organizations just throw in all the minutes of intervening committee meetings and then add insult to injury by having the chairperson read the minutes.

Don't expect that every board member is going to read everything, though if the material is effectively digested beforehand you'll be surprised at how many will. People who have a particular interest in a selected subject will carefully prepare for the discussion. Adopt the approach that you assume people have read the material in advance of the meeting. The presentations and discussions should start with that assumption and it should become an embarrassment for anyone to ask questions or make comments which clearly indicate that they have not done their homework.

Carefully identify the reason for each item's being on the agenda. Certain items will be there for important information purposes. Other items will be there for the board's consideration and disposition. One can't accurately predict what items will get fast action and which ones will require extensive debate. You may recall Parkinson's rule that the smaller the item the greater the attention it will be given. He uses the example of the board which quickly passes on the purchase of a multimillion-dollar nuclear reactor and then gets hopelessly bogged down in a discussion of purchasing garbage cans. He says that everybody knows about garbage cans and thus feels comfortable displaying this expertise.

Provide a suggested timetable. This obviously will be adjusted according to the board's interest, but at least it will provide some indication of the items which seem to require fuller consideration.

The board agenda and resource material should include intelligible financial reports, including an income and expense statement, balance sheet and budget status report.

Limit the executive director's report. For example, only occasionally do I make a report to the Board of Directors. I consider that if my job is properly done, the reports of the various committees, task forces and other officers will cover all the business that needs attention. (This is in keeping with my conception of the role of staff in voluntary organizations in which staff exists to assist the volunteers to carry on the mission and projects of the organization.) Occasionally there are management considerations or special observations I may want to share with the board. It's my impression that if I do not constantly dominate the board discussions, then the items or arguments I *do* bring to the board will carry more weight. I shudder at the meetings I go to where the executive director and other staff members carry the ball so totally and with such jargon and institutional shorthand that the board members are left glassy-eyed, limp and completely uninvolved.

LOCAL ANNUAL MEETINGS

It's probably accurate to say that most Annual Meetings are dinner meetings and that by the time the group is finished with the meal, the reports, the elections, the outgoing president's comments, the incoming president's comments, the awards, and the responses of those honored with awards, those members still present are absolutely numb, disengaged, and dreading the speech which is still to come.

Annual Meetings should be exciting and stimulating, and provide a significant thrust to the organization's major business. For these reasons, the basic rules governing all meetings which were given in the first few pages of this chapter are particularly important. Review them almost as a checklist. In addition, here are some other considerations which it is important to observe:

• Treat the Voting Membership as an important part of your organization. The Annual Meeting is a terribly important time for the Voting Members to be involved and informed about your future plans.

• Provide enough time for what needs to be done. If you really line up all that can (and should) be done at the Annual Meeting, it is almost a certainty that it can't possibly be reduced to a dinner meeting unless, as is too often the case, you are prepared to go on well into the night, thus making a deadening time of it for everyone concerned. Instead, given enough advance notice, people will set aside a Saturday or a weekday or at least an afternoon topped by a really fun-filled and interesting dinner without all the business being jammed and crammed in. To do this *(1)* adopt a time schedule and stick to it; *(2)* leave time for questions, discussion and debate; and *(3)* provide an advance agenda with written reports. (Include information on award winners, Nominating Committee recommendations, and summaries of the actions called for.)

• Relate the meeting to the basic thrust of the group. It's surprising how often organizations will choose themes and speakers which do not really fit into or contribute to the mainstream of their current efforts. It's almost as though Annual-Meeting Committees were divorced from the basic organization. Too often the pattern is to come up with a catchy theme and a principal speaker without regard to the tremendous opportunity presented to use this Annual Meeting as an occasion to really push the organization's basic projects.

• Plan carefully for awards and recognition. The Annual Meeting is a time when an organization can honor those who have served its cause. Be careful, though, not to present so many awards that the meaning is diminished. The awards can be listed in a printed program. In some cases, many people may be included in an award category; for instance, volunteers who have contributed more than 100 hours to the organization. These people can be asked to stand up as a group. If you are trapped into doing everything at a dinner meeting, present some of the awards in advance and then be sure their names are listed in the printed program. It's also effective sometimes to spread the awards throughout the agenda so that there isn't a bunching. Except in unusual cases, don't introduce individuals who aren't present. I always have a sinking feeling when names are called and people asked to stand and it turns out that several of the people aren't present.

• Select interesting locations. It's not always possible to come up with an imaginative approach, but people do like to visit an interesting place. This can be either a new hotel or, at the other extreme, a facility which relates to the agency's work. Be careful about the expense, however. Increasingly, agencies are involving youth and the poor, and those eight-dollar dinner tabs have a way of saying we don't really mean it. Consider, for a change, holding the meeting in a jail, state hospital, ghetto church, campground, new synagogue, a mansion donated for the day, a community college, a movie theater or legitimate playhouse, or even in city hall, a company's training facility, or any other place that's different, interesting, inexpensive, and perhaps educational.

• Work hard at promoting attendance. There should be early mailings to the Voting Membership, and to a very carefully developed list of outside groups and individuals. A *personal invitation* should be extended by officers and members of the Annual-Meeting Committee to the fifty outside people you are most eager to have present. It should be made very clear that the board members are expected to be there. Voting Members should also know they are expected to attend this one meeting each year. Committee members are part of the Voting Membership and they should be particularly urged to take advantage of this opportunity to get a broader feel of the organization. Promoting attendance requires imagination and hard work, but the Annual Meeting can be a very significant event in terms of public exposure, community involvement and agency thrust. There should be some members of the Annual-Meeting Committee carrying on an extensive telephone campaign to the board members, Voting Members, committee members, and others to promote attendance and get commitments.

• Take advantage of your publicity opportunities. Some of your promotion efforts can be assisted by advance notices to the news media. However, these will simply support your promotion efforts and should not be considered as doing the promotion job itself. The many events which will be part of a really good Annual Meeting will provide many pegs for advance stories and for news media coverage during the meeting itself.

• Spread the workload. One of the reasons that Annual Meetings often don't achieve their potential is that the event is left largely to the staff. However, it's the kind of activity which many board members will work very hard at. The Annual Meeting should be a major volunteer responsibility. The committee should be a year-round operation with regular reports to the Board of Directors. The various assignments, involving publicity, registration, promotion, awards, and program should be assigned to individuals or subcommittees. Obviously, staff backup is needed, but not nearly so much as we generally think is needed. Clearly, the opportunity and responsibility to make the most of this annual event should not be curtailed because staff doesn't have enough time. Most of the responsibilities can be carried by volunteers.

• Pay special attention to arrangements. What was said earlier about Murphy's Laws is doubly applicable to Annual Meetings. "What can go wrong will go wrong." Make a careful list of all the physical arrangements and doggedly check them through. If you don't, things will rapidly go wrong and Murphy's second law will come into play: "If unattended to, the situation will only get worse." Among the many things that can go wrong will be at least one of the following:

> —the microphone or speaker system won't work (or will squeal so badly that people will think they're experiencing a lobotomy),
> —the awards will be in the wrong order (or else they won't get there at all),
> —the president will introduce the head table from left to right when it's set up right to left,
> —the hotel will serve pot roast on Good Friday.

• Work hard at producing good meetings. They're the key to upgrading volunteer participation.

9.
Fund Raising

Almost every agency needs money. This applies to fledgling organizations, groups in search of new sources of funds, United Way affiliated organizations which need to supplement their income through self-support, and many other organizations which just plain need to raise money to support their existing programs or to enable them to carry out their plans for expansion.

If you are in a new organization, don't overlook the possibility of United Way support. Increasingly, United Ways are setting aside funds to help launch emerging organizations. Even if the United Way can't assist you at this time, their fund-raising experience can be of assistance in providing valuable tips for you.

Fund raising is awfully hard work, but if you have a cause that deserves support and you're willing to scratch, kick and beg, you can raise money. Fund raising has to be very high on your board's or Organizing Committee's priorities, however, and it must remain high in status and recognition within the organization. This is not easy. If you're reading this and wondering how to get moving, you probably already know the problem of a Board of Directors or Organizing Committee not really recruited with fund-raising responsibilities distinctly in mind. And if you're already getting most of your support from fees, contracts or United Way, it's even harder to stir up real fund-raising activity. Raising money takes dogged persistence, bull-headedness, salesmanship, year-round cultivation, board support and encouragement, a plan, an attainable goal, and lots of excitement.

One of the first obstacles that the doubters and foot-draggers will put in your way is that they will insist that the organization first has to develop more visible programs before it can win increased support. This is a myth and an excuse. You can raise money the first few times around with a cause and with promises. If the board decides it is going to raise more money and is willing to allocate at least 20 per cent of its energy and resources to accomplish it, you can succeed.

HEART ASSOCIATION EXPERIENCE

It's fascinating to hear people today speak about the American Heart Association's success. They automatically assume that the organization couldn't help but succeed. They will go on at great length about the fact that the organization had a visible cause, it had leadership, it had fund-raising staff, it had dollars to invest, it had a basic fund-raising blueprint, that the total association was organized and dedicated primarily to raising funds, and that, in the early Fifties, there was a wide-open climate for fund raising.

The fascination is to have been there more than twenty years ago and to know how similar the real picture was to that faced by most organizations today that are trying to figure out how to raise money at the local level. There wasn't a visible cause; we all decried the fact that a heart attack victim looked so normal that there was no chance to get the kind of sympathy you could generate with a poster showing a child polio victim. We didn't have leadership; certainly we didn't have the community leaders with us. Most of the leadership were physicians, who took little interest in fund raising. We didn't have a fund-raising staff—most of us were young do-gooders interested in learning something about community organization. We didn't have very many dollars, certainly not the kind of money necessary to prime the pump of a major campaign. We didn't have a blueprint for campaigning; indeed, we were floundering around trying to figure out whether to develop and sell valentines or go into the United Way; raise money by mail or accept government grants. And the organization certainly didn't have a fund-raising determination. In terms of fund-raising climate, everywhere we went we were told that people were tired of working, fed up with being asked to contribute, and that we should look to the Community Chest for support. It was terribly difficult to get local groups interested in fund raising and convinced that they could do it.

In just twenty-five years the Heart Association has gone from that beginning to an annual income approximating $60 million.

What evolved during the Fifties was, first, that officers and staff were convinced that money had to be raised, then gradually came the recruitment of campaign chairpersons who were willing to join up and give it a try, the evolution of the telephone recruitment method for door-to-door campaign volunteers, the development of the memorial gifts program, and a growing pervasive spirit for making each February's totals better than the February before.

As often happens, the darkest days turned out to provide some very real blessings. Throughout the Fifties, the American Heart Association was fighting for its life to survive growing United Way determination to take the association in or else to dry up its income sources. We lost a good many chapters, and we lost a great many board members. Indeed, we seemed to lose most of the bigger names we had tried so hard to recruit. It turned out, however, that those who stayed with us were a hardy lot. Contrary to belief, they were not often the significant community leaders. They were independent souls who were not frightened away and, by standing up and being counted, brought a verve, backbone and determination to that agency which has been its true making.

The American Heart Association has rapidly grown, expanding its income and its sources of funds. Its 1974 income profile looked like this:

Special Gifts	$3,423,958
Business	6,346,405
Door to Door	14,417,362
Special Events	3,321,789
Memorials	9,187,014
*Other Income	7,901,112
Bequests	14,085,522
Nat'l Office Direct Income	237,807
GRAND TOTAL	$58,920,969

* *Other—includes Federal services, mail, United Funds, coin containers, etc.*

I often think of those lonely early years, particularly when I hear all the same reasons why it can't be done today.

HOW TO GET STARTED

Let me repeat that you're in for some awfully hard work. I don't say this to discourage you. Indeed, I hope you'll push on. But if you're timid or your organization isn't really determined, you won't survive the obstacles and heartaches and difficulties which, unfortunately, I can promise you are ahead. On the other hand, let me repeat my earlier statement that if you have a cause that deserves support and if you're willing to scratch, kick and beg, you *can* raise money.

The procedure of getting started should be something like this:

• Convince the board or your fellow organizers to make a full commitment.

• Define the need. This doesn't have to be in any elaborate brochure, but define why you need money and try to come up with a needs goal. This shouldn't be "pie in the sky," but it shouldn't be too timid, either. What does your group really think it would actually need as a minimum to make a significant difference in the next three to five years?

• Develop a fund-raising plan. Basically, a plan involves the following:

a. An identification of the type or types of fund raising to be undertaken. On the basis of consultation with other agencies, persons who have been involved in fund raising in the community, and any consultants available to you from a parent organization, you will begin to get an idea of where your immediate potential rests. Don't scatter your shots too widely, but, as they say, don't put all your "begs in one askit," either!

b. Establish a realistic goal for the first year. Don't shoot immediately for your needs goal unless you have an angel or two in the wings or unless your needs are very, very modest. Set a goal that is attainable based on the sources of funds and the number of campaign workers it is going to be possible to recruit. Start small! Most campaigns tend to fall apart because the initial efforts are so ambitious as to be totally beyond the capacity of the organization. If a group becomes discouraged the whole effort quickly falls apart. On the other hand, if you set an attainable goal—and I don't mean that it has to be unduly modest—and you hit it, the organization will, in spirit and in fact, be on its way.

c. Determine exactly how many campaign workers you need to make the contacts necessary to raise that amount of money. Here, too, be coldly realistic. Determine the deployment of these campaign workers in terms of teams and the consequent need for captains and other leaders. Break the job down into bite sizes. Campaigns easily fall apart because unrealistic burdens are placed on too few people who either won't accept the jobs or don't follow through.

d. Set a firm timetable for recruitment, training sessions, campaigning, reporting and recognition. It will be terribly important to provide enough time to do the job. This doesn't mean that things can't be pulled together in a hurry but, if you're totally unreasonable, you just won't have time to do the job.

e. Decide on the budget. It needn't cost an arm and a leg, but the campaign is going to cost some money, and you have to be prepared to budget for the operation. If the budget won't cover what you're trying to do, you may be able to get some seed money from a corporation or individual.

• Bring the plan back to the board or the organizers to get their firm support, including approval of the budget, dollar commitments of support from individual board members, and guarantees of service. You may find at this point that some of the organizers and board members fall away, and you'll need to adjust your plans accordingly. Even though it's discouraging, it's better to have some shaking down at this point so that those remaining are as committed as you are to getting the job done.

• Recruit the chairperson. This is the most critical step. He or she needn't necessarily come from within the organization but should be someone who has a *demonstrated* capacity to accomplish the plan. Beware of talkers and, above all, don't seek a fast sell. This is one of the most important recruitment jobs you'll ever do. Talk to agency volunteers and staff. Talk to ministers and priests and rabbis. Talk to editors and successful business people. And talk to others who really know who produces. Keep your sights glued on such people!

• Establish and keep to a regular schedule of training sessions and report meetings.

• Provide for recognition and awards.

• Put some of the best of the campaign volunteers on the board.

• Develop your second-year plan, with heavy involvement of those who participated in the first success.

This all sounds very pat, and I certainly don't mean to suggest that, if one is willing to follow these steps, the success is assured. However, there's a much better chance of getting there if this kind of proven pattern is followed.

Right from the start you'll wonder where you're going to find the volunteers to carry on the campaign. The answer is that your volunteers are out there, but you've got to scratch hard to find them. People want a cause and are willing to join up if you can only reach them.

There have been many times when I've gone into a community absolutely cold and have succeeded in recruiting a campaign chairperson. My pattern is to go to priests, ministers and rabbis, the mayor, the head of a service club, heads of women's groups, and persons who have worked in other campaigns. I ask them if they can identify people who may wish to take on the kind of job I have outlined, and it is rare that this pattern does not produce a chairperson. Each prospect I talk to, I ask to be willing to help the chairperson who is finally recruited; so that even if I get several turn-downs, my chances are usually improved because I've got a growing cadre of helpers already lined up.

You've really got to look first to your Board of Directors for help, but through sad experience I know that if someone on the board has not already come forward, the situation is not likely to change. However, go over the list carefully to be sure that many of them are lined up to help.

Actually, the chairperson will be the kind who can do a good deal of his or her own recruiting, but don't leave your recruit all alone out on the limb. He or she can only give so much time, and since each chairperson *is* only one person, if you're going to make as large a step as possible in the first year, you're going to have to have a lot of helpers. Look to persons who have been helped by the organization or to people who have shown some interest in the cause. If the jobs are, in fact, bite-size, more people will be willing to help and will produce.

Don't sign up total organizations. This is a standard pitfall that it is essential to avoid. People will say that they can get this women's group or that men's group to take on the project, but it rarely turns out that way. Welcome opportunities to talk to the groups to enlist specific recruits, but don't count on another organization to do your organization's work. There are exceptions, of course, but the experience is generally unfavorable.

DO YOU NEED STAFF?

Many organizations raise goodly sums without staff. Don't underestimate how much can be accomplished without paid help. If, however, you are aiming toward a fairly sophisticated campaign involving many fund-raising categories with annual goals of $25,000 or more, you'll probably need staff help. This doesn't have to require a full-time trained fund-raiser, but you will have to be certain that someone can devote a realistic portion of time to the job and that the individual is willing to dive into it with enthusiasm and commitment and a willingness to learn.

Look to smart, young, aggressive women who may want part-time employment. You'll be surprised how much experience and ability are already out there in the community. Talk to other agency volunteers and staff, your United Way, and to community leaders who have been identified with major causes—they may be able to lead you to the right person.

Don't overlook the placing of advertisements in local

publications, but ask for written resumés to be sent to a blind box number so that you're not put under undue pressure by a great many people, including "friends."

Don't expect the staff person to be the campaign chairperson or to function in place of key volunteer figures. Staff exists only to help the volunteers carry out the work of the organization. If you turn too much of the load over to staff, the results are bound to be disappointing. It's the kind of volunteers you have in the campaign who are going to make the difference and, if they have some staff backup, they can make even greater use of the time they give.

Generally, I advise associations not to engage fund-raising firms to serve as staff for ongoing community campaigns. Many of these groups can be very helpful in developing fund-raising plans and most of them are expert at conducting capital gifts campaigns. Specialty firms and specialty departments of the larger firms are often skilled in direct mail solicitation, bequest cultivation, church "every member" drives, special events, and many other fund-raising categories. As such, they raise a great deal of money for voluntary organizations. I have tremendous respect for the ability of fund-raising firms, notably those associated with the American Association of Fund Raising Council. The only fund-raising role I've generally found them not particularly suited for is staffing the annual community campaigns of such groups as the voluntary health agencies. Many of the fund-raising firms with whom I've worked are the first to point out that they are not geared to provide this service. Their experience and professionalism make them more expensive than most local groups can afford on a regular basis and most local voluntary agencies don't have at hand or in early prospect sufficient community leadership to raise the sums which would justify the fees these firms have to charge.

I also generally discourage groups from hiring a person whose full-time job is working part-time for several agencies. I'm sure I'm doing some able people a disservice by saying this, but I must say that this arrangement so rarely works well in my experience, that I have to advise against it.

Build into your five-year campaign plan a firm estimate of staff needs and as soon as you can go to your own full-time person, make the switch. This may be hard on the individual whose part-time efforts have brought you to that happy transition, but if you're going to grow and sustain the momentum, you will need an individual who is good and is employed full time.

FUND-RAISING COSTS

Fund raising doesn't have to cost much money, but raising money does involve certain costs. Most of the costs are the staff time applied to the fund-raising operation. It's usually only the very small campaigns or the very large campaigns which can keep costs below 10 per cent. It's the middle area that becomes more expensive. Indeed, if you need staff, but are not at the point where you are attracting large gifts, the cost of the operation will almost have to be greater than 10 per cent. This isn't unethical and shouldn't shock or deter anybody. I don't know of a firm rule of thumb, but my own gut reaction is that an ongoing campaign is ethical and justified if its costs are one-third or less. If this means that your agency is able to raise a lot more money than it otherwise would and this means a greater pursuit of its public mission, then most givers will accept the morality and logic of that. Some initial campaigns will cost even more. Direct mail campaigns usually are a wash-out the first year, but if the field tests safely project that by the third year your renewals will be at a level so that your costs are down to the one-third level, I'd encourage you to go ahead. I've been involved in initial community campaigns that cost 50 per cent. It bothered me but, on the other hand, I knew that this was necessary to get the operation going and I knew that subsequent years' costs would drop to well below one-third.

In some campaigns involving sales of goods, the costs may routinely run above 50 per cent. This is all right so long as the givers are aware and satisfied that they are at one and the same time getting something they want and helping a cause. It's not fair if people are pressured into taking something they don't want or if the impression is left that most of the money will be going to charity. In some sales efforts, however, most of the money does go to charity, particularly if the sales items are donated.

THE PUBLIC-EXPOSURE VALUE OF CAMPAIGNS

Without getting deeper into the debate of how much public education is accomplished in fund-raising campaigns, it's at least obvious that the larger the campaign, the more public awareness there is of the cause. This helps in recruitment and also helps the organization to be identified as a source of help for the cause involved. It's my own belief that the benefits do, in fact, affect the program pursuits of the organization. I am convinced that 15 to 20 million persons involved in the American Cancer Society and American Heart Association campaigns over the past twenty years means that those individuals feel some identification with these causes. They have probably read some of the educational material and, because they identify with the groups, they also know where to turn when information or help is needed.

The fact of an annual campaign provides impetus for telling the association's story, and this is almost always very healthy for the organization. Even if it's only a membership effort conducted by an agency involved in the United Way, still this is an opportunity to remind a growing number of people *who you are, what you represent, what you can do for them, and what they can do for you.*

SUSTAINING THE EFFORT

Fund-raising campaigns can be fun. They are almost always exciting. They provide a rallying point for the organization and in many ways lend an air of excitement to the whole operation. They're also hard work! And sustaining the effort year in and year out is particularly tough. You'll need to carefully and quickly promote volunteers up through the campaign organization (and surely from the campaign organization to the board) so that there can be new blood and fresh leadership moving forward to share in the excitement of the campaign and thus be stimulated to carry the burdens of it for a while.

You must constantly seek ways to make clear to the workers how much their efforts mean. When I was with the American Heart Association in Baltimore, every year we sent a New Year's card to every one of the seven thousand block workers with a message something like this:

> *During the Season of Good Will toward Man we want to Thank You again for your Wonderful Service to your community as a Heart Association Volunteer*

Make it clear that one of the basic responsibilities of the campaign chairperson is to help recruit a replacement. Make it clear, too, that this is also one of the president's basic responsibilities. Place the responsibility firmly at one place or the other, but make it clear that the other has got to stand ready to help and to see that it happens.

Fund raising has to be high on the board's agenda and high in status and recognition within the agency. A successful fund-raising performance has to be acknowledged and applauded throughout the organization. Find every possible way to say "thank you" and to give people the warm feeling of accomplishment to which they are entitled and which all human beings desire.

People want a cause. You have to help your people realize that they've got an awfully good one which is not only doing great things but also is grateful for the campaign volunteers' efforts.

10.
Where Is the Money?

In 1974, according to *Giving U.S.A.* published by the American Association of Fund Raising Counsel, Inc., Americans gave almost $25 billion to more than 500,000 nonprofit institutions and agencies. About 85 per cent of the money came from individuals, and it's fascinating to note that of this amount, the overwhelming proportion came from individual contributors with annual incomes of $15,000 or less. This clearly represents good news for you, because it tells you that you probably have a potential among the broadest possible pool of citizens in your community. Among health and social welfare-type causes, most of the funds come from that large pool of individual contributors, either through direct gifts or through payroll deductions.

The next most important sources of support are bequests (12 per cent), foundations (10 per cent), and corporations (approximately 4 per cent).

WHAT ACTIVITIES SHOULD BE CONSIDERED?

Individual causes and organizations differ so much that it isn't very helpful to try to lead you on this. All I can really do is to present some of the categories so that you at least get a feel of the possibilities. It will be terribly important to work closely with the kinds of groups mentioned in the previous chapter in the development of your own campaign plan, including the specific categories that you desire to pursue.

1. *Special Gifts.* This is a pretty sophisticated kind of fund raising, and it may strike you as unusual for me to mention it first. It's been my experience, however, that you can often go to well-to-do people or to community foundations or corporations with a specific plea for leadership gifts or start-up grants. I've seen a number of organizations go to ten or fifteen such sources and ask for $500 a year from each for two years as a means of getting this kind of campaigning started. This of course means, automatically, that you are going to have to replace this money with new gifts at the end of two years, but that is part of your gamble.

Beyond leadership or start-up gifts, you may well find that there are upper-income families who may surprise you by having quite an interest in your cause. Carefully develop your list and be certain these people are seen personally. There will be a great temptation to say that a personalized letter going to 500 such people is better than trying to see ten or fifteen personally, but don't you believe it!

Your campaign plan can include a growing list of such personal contacts each year so that, at the end of five years, you will have a fairly sophisticated special gifts campaign launched.

2. *Community and Family Foundations.* An experienced executive of an older organization or a trust officer can

quickly identify the likely community and family foundations. These should be approached for leadership gifts or start-up grants, though some may be willing to provide an annual gift for several years and others may be willing to make at least a small contribution. Don't be timid—go to see them and tell them your story. Your knees may be knocking and your heart may be pounding and your hands may be shaking, but still your conviction will come through, and this is what often tips the scales.

Obviously if there is a member of the campaign organization who knows some of the individuals involved, this assistance should be used to its fullest extent—both as a door opener and to help sell the cause. In these categories, as in all categories, don't assume that someone won't give. Remember the story of Vivian Beaumont, who gave one of the major buildings which now stand in the Lincoln Center complex in New York. With dismay, one of her friends asked her why she had given her money to Lincoln Center and not to another theater with which the friend was identified, and Vivian Beaumont's surprised reply was, "Because they asked me!"

3. *Door to Door Solicitation.* Door-to-door campaigns are still one of the fastest means of raising substantial sums of money. You don't have to organize the whole community or region, you can start with certain neighborhoods. If I had to go from point zero to the maximum dollars in the shortest possible time, I would use the door-to-door campaign as the heart of my effort.

You can generally find women who have had experience with this kind of campaign who are willing to advise you—if not assist you—and they can often lead you to someone who will take on the task. There are many women who have had practical experience with door-to-door campaigns. Don't get too ambitious the first year—you'll begin to have dollar signs in your eyes when you think of the potential of reaching every house and when you hear what the American Cancer Society is raising by this method. If you are too ambitious to start with, the operation will collapse and it will be all the harder the next year. Decide what part of the community you can realistically tackle the first year and be satisfied to bite off just that much, with the assurance that there will be another year.

4. *Businesses.* Most businesses are tied closely to the United Way, but some will be willing to provide leadership or start-up gifts to deserving causes.

5. *Labor Groups.* Don't overlook the labor organizations. They have a history of significant generosity to worthwhile causes and may be quite sympathetic to helping a struggling new organization or to help launch a new effort by an existing organization.

6. *Special Events.* Special events are probably the most ubiquitous of American's fund-raising efforts. Special events are going on almost all the time and almost everywhere. These events involve balls, bake sales, golf tournaments, walkathons—an almost endless list of projects. Rather than go into all that here, let me urge you to get a copy of the book *Handbook of Special Events for Nonprofit Organizations* published by Association Press. This comprehensive manual will give you a good overview of all the kinds of fund-raising events that are possible.

My own approach is usually to get clubs and organizations to put on special events for the cause. It's better to have many organizations putting on special events rather than having your association itself trying to develop events. All this generates considerable publicity and attention which can lead to some gifts from the treasuries of the various organizations and to some volunteers from them.

Special events may well have a prominent place in your

initial campaign plan as one of the fastest means of making some money. I'd be inclined to caution you, however, about major dependence on any one special event. In the long run they have a way of wearing out and ending up being a somewhat fickle source of ongoing support. There are, of course, magnificent exceptions, but generally these are rarities and any one special event is not a secure way of funding an ongoing operation.

7. *Tag Days and Canister Collections.* In many communities tag days and personal canister solicitation are now prohibited or at least discouraged. It's also increasingly difficult to get people to do these chores, but it is still a useful way in which to raise money in a relatively short time. If you can get permission to have people with canisters stationed at major sports events and other affairs or if you can arrange to have a solicitation at movie theaters, these are still very good forms of money raising.

8. *Testimonials.* Many organizations use the testimonial approach. Some organizations raise a great deal of money this way and are able to sustain the operation. Most organizations, however, find it a means of raising immediate money for a special situation without the expectation that like sums can be generated each year.

The approach is to identify an individual who is esteemed and who deserves the honor. It's also necessary to pick someone who is sufficiently revered, feared or so central to peoples' economy that they will be willing to pay twenty-five dollars or more to come and honor him or her. These are usually dinners, and the emphasis is on selling tables to organizations, business associates and others who are eager to participate in the testimonial.

9. *Retail Sales.* Many organizations raise money through the sale of cookies, apple butter, flowers, magazines, aprons, Christmas cards, and a myriad other objects.

This can be an expensive proposition, so go into it with your eyes wide open. Many commercial groups will actively enlist your participation in selling their products, with a part of the profit going to your organization. Some of these efforts can be very helpful to organizations, but generally they are primarily helpful to the companies promoting the idea.

10. *Media Appeals.* Unfortunately, direct appeals for money through public media announcements have pretty much worn themselves out. Very little money is raised this way except for emergency or unusually dramatic appeals. It's almost certain that someone in your organization will suggest that this is the solution to your troubles, but I warn you that, though it will provide useful publicity, it probably will not provide significant income.

11. *Direct Mail.* Direct mail has proven to be a very useful source of income for many organizations. A direct mail approach usually requires a cause that has a broad appeal, but specialists can help zero in on an audience which fits your profile. This effort requires a very sophisticated professional direct mail specialist. You'll need money to have a field test done, and then if the field test is successful, you'll still have to expect that the first year will come close to a washout with expenses equaling income.

Direct mail tried through your own office to a wide constituency will not usually pay for itself. Many organizations have to discover this for themselves. It seems so natural that, with a cause as stirring as they believe theirs to be, people are bound to respond to a heartrending letter. It just doesn't happen that way.

12. *Memorials and Honorary Gifts.* Many organizations have successfully promoted memorial and honorary gifts. The American Heart Association has probably been the most successful in the area of memorial gifts. This falls

naturally in their direction because of the unfortunately high proportion of deaths caused by heart disease. In 1974 memorial gifts constituted $9 million, which was 15 per cent of the total American Heart Association income. Though it sounds terribly funereal, I find no delicate way to tell you that, if you're not in a death-related cause, memorials are not a likely source of substantial income. You may want to cite the success stories of some churches and synagogues, but I submit that their successes are grounded in their unique relationship to death.

Honorary gifts have been successfully promoted by many organizations. This takes very careful and long-term cultivation. It involves creating a habit among your own members and gradually among a widening circle of friends so that they automatically think of the honorary gift as a way of expressing special congratulations to people on the occasion of a birthday, baptism, marriage, bar mitzvah, anniversary or on holidays.

A growing number of people send a simple post card at Christmas indicating that, in lieu of many Christmas expenditures including Christmas cards, they have made a donation in the name of their friends to a particular charity.

13. *Membership.* Memberships represent a slow but very secure long-term source of support. In many campaign plans I've developed, such support starts low and rises steadily, while the special events category starts high but doesn't increase substantially. The membership dues should be at a high-enough dollar figure to provide for regular service of the members and support for the program. Five dollars is a minimum and, if possible, I go to ten or fifteen. Members should be recruited first from the board. Every board member should be at least a contributing member, if not a special giver. Then move to past board members, current committee members, and out to the per-

sons served by the agency, to persons who have shown an interest in the cause, and watch the circles expand. As many potential members as possible should be approached personally. Until you have a chance to recruit a very wide group personally, you may want to approach some of the more likely prospects by phone or mail. Some organizations have been successful in setting up membership booths at conventions and meetings of other groups.

Set a specific goal in terms of the eventual proportion of the population you want to enlist as members. For instance, a local Mental Health Association strives to enlist and hold a minimum of one-half of 1 per cent of the population. This gives an organization something very specific to shoot at, and the goal can be divided into annual targets.

In large operations which depend on thousands of members, the cultivation and maintenance of the membership becomes almost a science. This includes an accurate determination of who are the people who might have an interest, how do we reach them, what is our pitch, how much can we ask, and how do we hold their interest?

Remaining responsive to the members' interest is a central matter. At an early point, Common Cause experienced quite a fickle membership until it realized that some members joined up when one kind of program was being pushed and fell away when the organization moved on to a new priority in a different field. When Common Cause realized that its central mission and the central interest of the largest pool of potential members was to make government more effective and more responsive to voters, for whatever the issues, the organization stabilized and began to experience more even growth.

Recently I was asked to react to a Task Force Report which attempted to plot the rebirth and future of a national agency. My advice zeroed in on this basic matter of constituency:

"The major observation and largest question I have about the Task Force Report deal with the need to give far more attention to identifying the constituency and financial base. I realize the report anticipates that temporary funding can be obtained to carry the operation for the next three years, but I submit that many of the decisions made now will govern what continuing support will be generated to carry it beyond three years. Under other parts of my comments I'll be returning to the essentiality of identifying and serving a constituency, but I think it is the basic *prior* question to which the Task Force must address itself. I, and most community organizers, have learned the hard way that one can't simply assume that, if one does good, support will be forthcoming. The agency needs to know what cause it wishes to serve, who are the constituents who want that job done, and what are the kinds of things that these groups will pay for. Unless these things are closely defined, there can't then follow a systematic dogged cultivation of those constituents and that support. It will likely follow, also, that without a pretty clear understanding of the audience, an agency can find itself orchestrating a pretty diverse program which may make sense to the players but won't excite or hold the subscribers."

BEQUESTS

The fastest-growing source of donated funds is bequests. Bequests now constitute 12 per cent of American giving. This is almost $3 billion.

Bequest cultivation is a very sophisticated form of fund raising and obviously cannot be counted in your short-term fund-raising plans. For organizations that are building long-term fund-raising projects, however, a realistic proportion of the effort should be reserved for bequest cultivation.

Several years ago I was able to bring an unusual group together to provide guidelines for what I wanted to be a very serious, major, and successful bequest promotion for a local chapter of the American Heart Association. The group was assembled by the chief judge of the probate court and included other probate judges, trust officers of major financial institutions, and tax and estate lawyers. All were assured that they would not have direct fund-raising responsibility, but would only provide a blueprint for the organization to follow. As so often happens when a group gets involved and interested, we were able to successfully recruit several of the individuals, not including the judges, to lead the implementation.

In a series of three meetings chaired by the chief judge, the group produced the following blueprint which was followed and which very shortly began to provide very substantial legacies. In the intervening years, the program has produced almost staggering results with surprisingly little effort.

1. *Basic Assumptions*
   a. That a very small proportion of the Bar writes 75 per cent of the wills that include gifts to charity.
   b. That these lawyers are almost always community figures or seen by their clients as important in the community.
   c. That most people who have money to leave are not certain which charities to consider.
   d. That lawyers who are community leaders are frequently asked by will-writing clients to suggest examples of worthy charities or asked if certain causes are really O.K.
   e. That a bequest cultivation program is not as long-range as might be assumed, because most people

write or amend wills when there is reason to be concerned.

f. That lawyers are interested and curious about heart disease.

g. That broad-scale mail campaigns with fancy brochures don't really make a dent.

2. *The Program Which Evolved*

a. We used several members of the original group to form our bequest cultivation committee.

b. The committee screened the names of the will-writing attorneys. (I learned that these can be pretty quickly identified by checking which lawyers in your community are members of the two relevant ABA sections dealing with taxation and estates.)

c. It turned out that there were approximately 170 such attorneys in a metropolitan area of approximately 2,000,000. We expanded our committee to include several more of the 170.

d. We held several meetings of the committee to help explain the problems of heart disease and the work of the American Heart Association.

e. Our basic approach was for every committee member to "adopt" twelve fellow will-writing attorneys. The assignment included:

(1) An initial luncheon or evening session. These we usually held at the committee member's club or home and with the purpose of outlining:

(a) Where do we stand in heart disease control?

(b) How can an individual protect himself?

(c) What is the American Heart Association?

       (d) A plan for future mailings.

    (2) Once each year thereafter the committee member sent a personal letter to the attorneys for whom he was responsible. The mailings included the current annual report and other progress reports.

    (3) The object was not hard-sell, but rather to be certain that the 170 will-writing attorneys were given a chance to know more about heart disease and the American Heart Association.

  f. One of the basic steps the committee recommended was that every member of the Board of Directors of the association should include a bequest, however small, in his or her will.

Even the long list of campaign categories covered in this chapter doesn't begin to cover all the possibilities, but it will give you some feel of the most likely things to be explored. I have not included any discussion of such devices as gift annuities, gifts of appreciated property, charity remainder trusts, and many other important sources of funds. These will generally not be applicable until you have built a corps of annual givers and committed supporters. For those who feel the need to explore these types of sophisticated solicitations, one of the best resources is Raymond Knudsen's *New Models for Financing the Local Church*, published by Association Press.

Don't try to tackle too many sources at once. When you finally decide which ones fit your organization, go after them with ferocious determination. Shake the dickens out of these sources and you'll find that the dollars will begin to multiply.

11.
The Importance of Communicating

Most of this book is about effective communications. Certainly much of the success of a citizens' organization depends on effective communications among the people who care and from them to the broader community which must be influenced. It seems important to pull together some aspects of the formal communications which are so essential a part of an organization's ability to operate and accomplish its mission. What do you know that others need to know in order to do their jobs effectively or at least to feel that they are a more integral part of the organization? In management lingo, the principle is stated as "the transmission of information exclusively possessed."

INTERNAL COMMUNICATIONS

One of the greatest problems of citizen organizations is that, in the limited time most people can give to a cause, they tend to become so wrapped up in participating that they don't take the time to adequately communicate to others who either need to know or who would find it fun to know.

Volunteering should be both exciting and purposeful —but this depends on being in the know and being involved. It's particularly important, therefore, that the leaders of the organization project themselves into the place of the people out there, and to do this often enough and fully enough to really grasp what they know that others need to know not only in order to be more effective participants but also to feel a keener sense of the mission and thrust of the agency.

If your operation is small enough, bring the full group together periodically just to be briefed on what's happening. As the undertaking grows, don't assume that you have to jump from personal communications to dull mimeographed reports. Whatever size the undertaking, devote a part of each meeting—subcommittee, committee, board or membership—to filling in your people on what's new. Sooner or later you'll have to add some regular written reports, but they really don't have to be deadly. Write them as though you were talking to people you like. Put yourself in their place and figure out what they'd really like to know. Focus on the cause and not the organization. You'll be preoccupied with organizational matters and when you begin to prepare for personal or written briefings your head will be full of the immediate concerns. Stop and clear your mind and concentrate on what the average member really cares about. If you're not good at writing reports or you find that you just can't ever seem to make time for them, ask someone else to take on this assignment for you. Many people enjoy this function and can do it well. Keep the charge simple: *What's happening that our people want to hear?*

There's another advantage to asking someone else to

help with newsletters and other written briefings. Most leaders know so much about a subject that they don't know where to begin—and particularly they don't know where to stop! They assume an utterly exaggerated degree of reader knowledge and interest. The only people worse at this than presidents are executive directors.

A briefing, as the name implies, should be brief, but make it easy for people to ask for more information. Such reports should also be frequent. Don't wait until you've got a slug of information to pass on. That is so overwhelming to the average members that most of them will just put such communications aside in that never-never-land pile we all call *later reading.* The test is not whether the communication is slick or has pictures, but whether we emphasize the *brief* in briefings and are on target with what our people really want to know. The larger the organization the more time that has to be carved out for communicating well. A voluntary association should strive to be personal and human.

I work very hard at trying to make my weekly memos to the field personal communications. I put in anecdotes, am constantly on the lookout for bits of humor, and I try to say things which let people know that I care about them enough to want to share some news. Though the memos go to hundreds, many of whom I haven't met, they are always signed just "Brian." Organizations so easily become cold and impersonal that every possible means must be used to counter those forces and to make things personal and human.

One of the devices I use to make written briefings as personal as possible is to write to specific individuals. With every chapter of this book I've had people in mind so that each part might come across as though I were talking to human beings. I've been trying to tell *you* something that I think *you* might want to know and to let *you* know I care enough to try to say things in a way that will add up to personal communication.

People who serve as leaders of voluntary organizations are in privileged positions. We are constantly hearing, reading, and doing things that are far more interesting than the experiences of the average person. Too often we are guilty of being in exclusive possession of this information and experience and we don't go through the exercise of squeezing the sponge to let others know what we know. One of the basic messages in all the orientation and training sessions in which I participate is this matter of "squeezing the sponge." I almost beg people to reflect on every day's experiences to determine what there has been that others need to know either in order to do their jobs better or would find fun in knowing. This can, of course, result in people telling a lot more than others really want to know. But if all this is combined with a discipline of "boiling it down," the information comes through in bite sizes and is manageable.

We all know the individual who sends us endless pages of speeches and reports, with the notation: "Every person in the organization will want to be familiar with. . . ." That's not fair. Decide what in all of that is in fact interesting and then boil it down. This discipline of "squeezing the sponge" and "boiling it down" is hard work. But we're pretty selfish if we sit in positions where we have opportunities to know things that others don't know and then don't take the trouble to pass along the part of it they really deserve to have.

It's hard work to make mailings personal and interesting. It's awkward at times to screen out items that others want to put in, but which, if included, will result in losing the flavor and the effectiveness of the mailings. For all these reasons most people either don't communicate or else they overcommunicate.

- Be on the constant lookout for human interest items —items that will help your members to have a good feeling about the work of the organization.

- Work hard at putting in some humor. Good Lord, life is dull enough for such a good part of the time that a little humor is always welcome.

- Don't always talk about problems. Voluntary agencies have such aspirations that the leaders are almost always preoccupied with the gap between performance and goals. Indeed, it's our job to be where the problems are so that the obstacles can be overcome and the progress restored. However, we shouldn't make everyone else suffer because of our problems. Work hard to keep your message spirited and positive.

- In this phase of organization, as in almost all aspects of management, the good operation is characterized by thoughtfulness and empathy. What do you know that others need to know either in order to do their job well or to feel they are a closer part of the operation?

- "Squeeze the sponge" and "Boil it down"!

EXTERNAL COMMUNICATIONS

People make news and your organization is people. Therefore, you are already halfway toward getting your share of the headlines.

When most of us think of news we still think about the daily newspaper. This is an important source to be cultivated, but consider some of the other print possibilities, too:

Neighborhood Newspapers. There are more and more community or neighborhood newspapers and they are hungry for news of people within the areas they serve.

Ethnic Newspapers. These newspapers are almost always worn thin from reading and the circulation is not incidental.

Industrial House Organs. Employees and their families do read the company house organ.

Speakers' Bureaus. Clubs and organizations are often eager to know what is going on in the community. If you've got a story to tell, you can reach an ever-widening group of significant community people through the use of speakers and films.

Company Mailers. Public utilities, banks and other companies will often include a brief printed message from your organization when they send out their bills and statements at the end of the month.

Bus Cards. You usually only have to pay for the cards. Sometimes you have to pay for the installation, but a lot of people ride public transportation and they have to stare at something.

Public Booths. In many communities you can still set up a booth downtown to pass out flyers.

Fairs. Most fairs still provide free space or low-rent space to public organizations. A lot of people attend state, county and other fairs.

Flyers. You may want to distribute flyers at public gatherings.

Skywriting. This may seem extreme, but truly the sky is the limit in the number of opportunities available to tell your story.

All of the above are important avenues to getting your story across. However, they are all involved in the print media, and while this is an important area to be pursued, it's only a part of the total possibilities open to you. Indeed, most voluntary agencies are still preoccupied with print media at the very time when more and more people are getting their information through audiovisual means. For instance, the above list doesn't include TV stations. You may feel intimidated by the mystery and aura of television, but the program and public service managers of the stations are constantly looking for community news. Radio and TV stations are required to devote a significant amount of their time to public service. You probably already know that radio has experienced a fantastic resurgence in the past ten years and today is a very important communication medium which should be in your plans.

Occasionally your organization may be involved in a public demonstration and this will provide an unusual opportunity for public exposure.

It's difficult to advise at this distance without knowing your particular needs, but I did want you to begin to get a feeling of the vast array of opportunities open to you. One of the reasons I do this is because most people are awed and scared off by the world of communication—with the result that they fail to realize how easy it is to find ways of getting their story across to the public.

A basic rule is to involve a person in your organization who knows what this communication game is all about. This should be a creative person whose job will be to constantly scrutinize the organization from the angle of "what's news?" Such volunteers are not one in a million, as you might think. One of the fortunate things is that there are many creative and experienced people in every community who welcome the opportunity to get their hand in. Look particularly for women who have had news media experience—radio or TV or newspaper. You can find these people by talking to ad agencies, television and radio station managers, newspaper editors and executives in other organizations. Incidentally, I've found that the best PR people represent a rare combination of creativity and attention to detail. They have the capacity to create stories, but they also know that most day-to-day publicity is achieved by grinding out the mundane information about committee appointments, speaking engagements, campaign progress, and the like.

One of the basic staples of news which is almost always overlooked, because people assume that the news media are too sophisticated, involves the announcement of appointments. These may no longer get such attention in the daily newspaper or on radio-TV, but this is the kind of information that community newspapers and company house organs are looking for. Whenever people are appointed to anything in the organization, ask them to fill out a standard form which includes the house organs, newsletters, community newspapers and ethnic newspapers they think might be interested. In many communities this can apply also to radio stations which specialize in community news.

Your creative public information person will find many ways to make the most out of occasions big or small—including the Annual Meeting, campaign kickoff, board meetings, special awards, your record of program activities, and an almost endless succession of activities and events which you might not even think of as newsworthy. In part, this is because you're not looking at the organization from the news media point of view or perhaps you are looking at the media only from the daily newspaper or TV point of view. Almost everything that the organization does will be of interest to one news medium or another.

It's important to tell our story to the communicators. We are usually so shortsighted that we constantly try to figure out how to tell our story to the general public and we overlook the communicators themselves. If our cause is worthy and our story is at all interesting, you will find that the news media representatives will be interested in hearing about it. This doesn't have to relate to any immediate news prospects but only that they are briefed on who you are and what you do. This will lead to significant benefits later and may even result in immediate suggestions of early coverage. Keep the communicators informed if you want to communicate to the public.

It's often useful to pull together a Public Information or Public Relations Committee. This won't usually operate in the structured way that most of our committees do. Instead, just by bringing together advertising people, media representatives, company people who purchase advertising space and time, and others, you can get good advice about how to make news. Also, you'll have some door openers who can help when and where it counts.

One of the most important means of external communication starts with internal communications. If you keep your membership well informed, and particularly if you give them a feeling of the agency's activities and exciting thrust, they'll be telling the story by word of mouth. It's particularly important to keep your Board of Directors and Voting Membership informed so that they can be spreading the word.

Sustaining public exposure is hard work. It requires dogged examination of what's happening and how those things can become media possibilities. This is why the basic step is to find the creative person who will have the job of constantly scrutinizing the organization from the angle of "what's news?"

12.
Budgeting
and Financial Accountability

By their very nature, voluntary associations operate with public support and therefore have a very real responsibility to spend that money judiciously and to report on its expenditure to the public.

In a speech entitled, "Responsibility of the Board Member of Voluntary Health Agencies," Marion Folsom, former Secretary of the U.S. Department of Health, Education and Welfare, said: "It is definitely the responsibility of the individual lay Board Members to insist that their agencies cooperate in this program. The businessman can be especially helpful here. He should be sure that his agency is determining the cost of each of its services and is giving complete information to the public."

STANDARDS OF ACCOUNTING AND REPORTING

An organization which handles more than $5,000 should have an audit, and therefore will be bound by the new accounting practices spelled out for the auditing profession in the *Audit Guide for Voluntary Health and Welfare Organizations* published by the American Institute of Certified Public Accountants. This guide is a companion piece to the *Standards of Accounting and Financial Reporting for Voluntary Health and Welfare Organizations* published by and available from the National Assembly, National Health Council and United Way of America. The foreword to the *Standards* says: "Adoption and use of the standards presented in this publication will enable voluntary health and welfare organizations to report their income and expenditures uniformly and in terms the contributing public can understand."

Even if your organization is not required to have an audit, it will pay to consult with an auditor to determine what requirements or practices you should observe to protect yourself, the organization, and the public.

In this chapter it will be assumed that your operation is sufficiently large to be audited and that there is probably a need to delineate the separate roles of the volunteer leader and a staff person.

The *Standards* are obviously important and will provide substantial benefits for individual agencies and the voluntary field in general. The *Standards* are appropriately designed to provide effective and uniform reporting to the public. However, they do not provide the basic information needed to effectively manage an agency. Thus, the system must be supplemented if a manager is to have the type of information needed to control and manage the agency.

For example, the *Standards* will provide the organization and the public with information about the organization's proportional expenditures in certain fixed functional categories such as community services and public health education, but the manager will need to know more specifically how the money is being spent within his agency for specific program functions. Within professional education and training, he'll need to know what has been spent for nurses seminars, traineeships, consecutive case conferences, and so on. The line items are also intentionally broad so as to apply to all voluntary health and welfare organizations, and in that regard, too, they have to be supplemented.

BUDGETS

Budgeting in voluntary agencies is always a frustrating process for financial and business people. One of the basic problems is that it's difficult to move back the timetable so that a realistic budget will be at hand well before the beginning of the fiscal year. The income of an agency is often so uncertain that it's difficult to forecast much before the end of one fiscal year and the beginning of another. Ideally, the closest one can come to an intelligent timetable is to have a budget prepared two or three months before the beginning of a fiscal year. Earlier projections are, of course, possible and often necessary for United Way presentations and other purposes, but generally a firm budget isn't in focus until very close to the beginning of the fiscal year.

Without getting into an exhaustive review of budget making, it might be useful to comment briefly on the process of developing income and expense projections. Usually, leaders of voluntary operations are so close to the cause and so overwhelmed with how much needs to be done that they will overestimate income and underestimate expenses. The hardheaded realism of the treasurer and the Finance Committee is essential as an offsetting influence.

Income projections should be based on a very practical and objective analysis of current sources of income, including a source-by-source and gift-by-gift review. This not only makes for practical budgeting but it also provides sensible preparation for the degree of work necessary to renew gifts and find new money. It's essential not to project substantial new income, or at least not to count on it, to cover fixed expenses. The usual approach for voluntary agencies is to hope so desperately for new income that we count it in the budget, and then, when it doesn't materialize, we end up with a deficit or horrendous cutback. The wiser approach is to have an opportunity for budget revision during the year to allow additions according to new income produced.

If you have staff, expense projections are also developed initially by the staff director. Here the incoming president should be carefully consulted and, of course, the treasurer and Finance Committee chairperson will be closely involved and will again provide a pragmatic influence.

It is important that the Finance Committee never be allowed the authority of making decisions which rightfully belong to the Executive Committee or the Board of Directors. Many Finance Committees, in their appropriate efforts to cut or control expenditures, will make decisions about what activities should stay or go, and this is beyond their authority. They may well say to the president, staff and board that their appraisal of income projections will not sustain the expenses budgeted. Then, if the board agrees with the Finance Committee's figures, it is up to the officers or board to decide where the cuts will have to be made.

The budget should be prepared early enough so that the full Board of Directors or at the very least the Executive Committee can be involved in its review and approval before the beginning of the fiscal year.

The format for the budget should include at least the following:

- A narrative summary of the year ending and the year ahead.
- A five-year review of income and expenses.
- A comparison of working fund activities and balances for the closing and prior years.
- A proposed budget including, for each line item, the prior year's budget, the prior year's actual, and the recommendation for the coming year.

You will note that a narrative summary is recommended. I worked with one treasurer for six years and we had a perfect relationship except once a year we would have our annual set-to over whether I would be allowed to do a narrative summary. This clashed with his banker's approach, but I knew the narrative was the only way that many board members would really grasp what the budget picture was all about.

One of the basic parts of the budgets I prepare is an estimated dollar value of the volunteer time contributed to the agency. This is always the first item in the budget itself. This helps put all the rest of the budget, and particularly staff salaries, into perspective. My goal is to constantly increase the ratio of contributed time to staff salaries. Though there is no comparison available, I feel that something close to a 10 to 1 ratio would probably represent effective use of volunteers in relation to staff time.

It's important to put a good deal of information into the budget, including the detailed breakdown of the various line items. For instance, within the line item of *employee costs,* it is important for the board members to know the relative costs of basic medical, major medical, retirement, social security, unemployment insurance, and any other benefits which might be provided. Most board members won't want to get into that much detail, but at least it's there. This is reassuring to all board members and is important to those who do want to get into detail.

Budgeting dollars is only part of the necessary budgeting process. Budgeting staff time is perhaps even more important. Just as dollar resources have to be carefully directed toward the priorities determined by the board, so too must staff time. This sounds much more complicated than it really is. It's simply a matter of identifying the number of staff weeks that are available for actual work and matching these to the ongoing activities and special projects. If time sheets are coordinated with this, it's very easy for a staff person to indicate the specific activities and projects to which time was devoted during the day. At the end of a month or quarter or year, it's possible to see if the staff time was actually spent in the patterns and on the priorities intended. This is an important way also to help board and committee members to better grasp the current level of commitments. Otherwise, in the absence of this kind of specific information, boards and committees are almost too ready to add new projects.

• Dollars and staff time are the two basic resources available to the volunteers, and both must be carefully measured and metered if they are to be directed in ways consistent with the agency's goals.

FINANCIAL STATEMENTS

An organization should produce a monthly income and expense statement, balance sheet, and budget status report. These should go to the Board of Directors and to the Executive Committee in advance of each of their meetings. Copies should also be sent monthly to the Finance Committee.

The audit should also go to the board with ample

opportunity for discussion. It's also a good idea to arrange to have the auditor meet with the Finance Committee so that this important group of board members really feel they know the financial picture, up to and including the auditor's appraisal of internal controls.

An agency with one or more staff members will often end up with three different kinds of statements: *(1)* those required in the *Standards;* (2) those developed for management purposes, and *(3)* additional statements in a format required by governmental bodies, the United Way or others.

I reconcile the requirements for different financial reports by starting with the system and information I need to manage the agency. I make sure that this is not incompatible with the *Standards,* and that my year-end reports can be easily recast into the format required by the *Standards.* Similarly, the records can be recast to provide special information required by the Finance Committee, governmental agencies and others. But the basic point is the need for a system which is conducive to sound day-to-day management.

In an understandable preoccupation with meeting the required accounting standards, too many agencies are trying to operate with the information that comes out of that system and it just isn't adequate.

INVESTMENTS

Operating and reserve funds which are available for short-term investment should be invested in savings accounts, certificates of deposit, treasury bills, and certain categories of commercial paper. They should not be invested in common stocks. This includes all funds which are needed for operations or which are considered ready reserves.

When common stocks are received as current contributions and are considered part of operating funds or ready reserves, they should be sold at time of receipt. If the organization is fortunate enough to have endowment funds, these funds should be managed by a major financial institution selected by the Finance Committee and approved by the Board of Directors. The investment policy should be established by the board. This can include a "Combined Income" or "Total Return" plan whereby the association, in consultation with the financial institution, establishes a fixed income which will be drawn from both income and principal. This allows for investment of some substantial part of the fund in common stocks as a hedge against inflation. The Finance Committee should do an annual review of the fund, and members of the Finance Committee should be readily available to consider special advice from the financial institution.

SOME HARD-EARNED LESSONS

In twenty years of voluntary agency administration, I have had some pretty rude awakenings and learned some pretty sad lessons. Let me summarize these lessons from the school of financial hard knocks.

• *Budget realistically.* It's too easy to get carried away with unduly optimistic income projections and unrealistic expectations. The resulting deficits and the pure horror of the budget cutbacks—particularly those which involve personnel—gradually teach the lesson that it's better to face reality and disappointment during the budgeting process than later.

• *It's essential to have regular monthly reports and to study these carefully.* These reports should include at very least the income and expense statement, balance sheet and budget status report. These should be carefully studied. A situation can change rapidly, and unless caught early the picture is simply not reversible.

• *Be sure the reports are really accurate.* This may seem terribly obvious, but I have lived with and through situations where, because of switchovers in accounting systems or problems of personnel in the accounting area, or just a plain poor accounting staff, reports have not been reliable. It's easy during these periods to assume that one has a close enough view of the organization to suppose that the reports are not far out of kilter. Don't you believe it! If there is any indication that the reports are not absolutely accurate, get that situation straightened out fast.

• *Insist on really understanding the financial picture and the reports.* It's better to be willing to look absolutely silly rather than not to pursue a part of the financial picture or report which you don't quite understand. It's not sufficient that the auditor understands it or the treasurer or the accountant. The president and executive director are the ones responsible for the operation, and *they* have to understand it. Staff should be sure the books are organized in such a way that they help the staff director manage. It's awfully easy to assume that by meeting the accounting standards or by supplying the Finance Committee with what it wants, there are enough financial reports and information floating around. Don't play to that tune. Get the books into a form that the staff director really understands and be sure they provide the basic information necessary to manage the agency. Do it in such a way that the figures can easily be recast to satisfy the other requirements or needs.

• *Establish a close working relationship with the auditor.* For the staff, day-to-day access to the auditor is essential. Provide a realistic sum in the budget over and above the cost of the audit so that the staff director can feel absolutely free to regularly consult with the auditor on many financial management considerations.

- *Involve the auditor in establishing, or at least approving, your internal systems, including controls.* It's not enough to assume that the auditor is absolutely satisfied with your systems and controls simply because he provides you with a *clean* audit. There may be too much that he's assuming, and, because this is such an essential area to be properly organized, it is wise to involve him in setting up the system or at least regularly tracing it through down to the most minute details.

- *Make the most of the interest and knowledge of the treasurer and chairperson of the Finance Committee.* Your treasurer and chairperson of the Finance Committee can help tremendously in interpreting agency operations and finances to the Board of Directors. They will be useful in handling short-term investments or helping line up bank loans during low cash flow. But, most of all, it will be their hard-nosed, pragmatic, conservative, fiscal judgment which you will need. They often provide unwelcome advice, but for that very reason it's all the more important to have it permanently at hand.

- *Involve the incoming president in the development of the budget.* The budgeting function is too often seen as an internal staff responsibility, but the person who will be serving as president when that budget will be in effect can feel left out or thwarted if he or she doesn't understand the budget and doesn't have an opportunity to mold it to help pursue priorities as the president and the board perceive them.

- *Recognize how easily the budget can thwart or contradict the board's decisions on priorities.* The board can go through an elaborate process of determining new priorities, and yet if the budget follows the same old pattern, the resources of dollars and staff are not likely to be converted to the new pattern of priorities.

- *Provide for some cushion in the budget.* I am not very good at this and yet I know from sad experience how important it is. It's so hard to cut a proposed budget back to fit realistic projections of income that I am almost never able to build in a 10 or even a 5 per cent cushion. On the other hand, I know that it is just not possible to anticipate fifteen months in advance what emergency and undeniable demands will occur in the following fiscal year. A budget should have a contingency factor of 5 to 10 per cent to be allocated, hopefully in small amounts, by the Executive Committee or Board of Directors for those emergency and unanticipated special needs which arise during the year.

• *Provide for some basic reserves.* Voluntary agencies should have reserves equal to at least one-half of one year's operating expenses, though not greater than one year's operating expenses. This provides funds during low cash flow, a cushion against the almost inevitable occasional deficit, and some breathing room for emergencies. All this, of course, in addition to the basic purpose of a reserve to help the agency survive a truly catastrophic period.

• *Don't switch accounting systems until you are really on top of your information.* There is always a temptation to help solve a current accounting problem by moving to a new system. My experience has been that you had better be very certain that you are getting accurate information from your current system before you start major adjustments. For example, I've seen a number of agencies run into terrible difficulty during a transition to computer operations. It's essential to be getting accurate information from your current system before and until the new system is accurately operating.

• *Voluntary agencies are never going to get rich.* Your people will sometimes wonder when that day will come when the agency won't be living hand-to-mouth or be facing an imminent financial crisis. I don't mean to unduly discourage you, but I don't think that the really effective voluntary agency dealing with a major public problem is ever going to be comfortable. The needs and pressures to do even more will always outweigh income. I've found that it's helpful to my mental health to finally realize this! At least I know it's a way of life and I'm not periodically disappointed that the tables haven't yet been turned.

- *Deficits are hell!*

13.
The Involvement of Minorities

This will be a short chapter. It's short because I don't pretend to have enough experience to tell anyone else how to do it. On the other subjects in this book I have put enough years in to have some license to talk, but on this one I'm scrambling to catch up. However, a book dealing with effective operation of contemporary voluntary associations which doesn't address itself, even inadequately, to the subject of involvement of minority groups is hardly a realistic effort.

DECIDE WHAT YOU MEAN TO DO AND IF YOU REALLY MEAN TO DO IT

It doesn't take very much experience to know this is not an area to tackle casually. Too much of the effort has been the product of starry-eyed do-gooders who wanted to help. A decision to effectively involve minorities is very serious business because, if it's done right, it's going to change your way of doing things. It's particularly important to conscientiously decide why you want to involve minorities and to have some reasonable knowledge of how you anticipate this will improve the organization's focus and activities. It's hard to criticize those who simply want to do it because it's right, but significant involvement will have such impact on the organization that you'd better be sure there is sufficient commitment to carry it to its ultimate conclusion.

Most of the lessons I'm finally learning relate to how an organization really translates a commitment into reality. There's also another lesson, which I'll speak about later, that says the organization, however well-intentioned about effective involvement of minorities, must also have a continuing sense of its own unique mission. If it doesn't, the new minority participants will quite naturally, and from their point of view quite logically, force the organization to respond to their agenda of very real social concerns. For all these reasons, this chapter begins with the urgent admonition: *Decide what you mean to do and if you really mean to do it.*

FINDING THE WAY TO BE OF SERVICE

My whole emphasis here is on effective *involvement* of minorities rather than on effective service *to* minorities because I've learned that the involvement has to come first if the resulting service is to be on target. Because that lesson is so central, let me tell you more about how I learned it. Several years ago a Board of Directors with which I was involved came up with a healthy resolve to pay more attention to the needs of minority groups and the poor. Among the first steps adopted was "to assemble a committee of advisors from among those most knowledgeable and involved in these areas to advise us on the implementation of these goals." Most board members assumed that this committee would come up with a series of projects which the organization could then undertake. If we had only applied our own community organization experience and some common sense to the issue at hand, we wouldn't have been so surprised by the committee's recommendations. In essence, they said that it wasn't possible or appropriate for any group of do-gooders, black or white, to decide what was good for other people and then to impose programs on them. The committee reminded us that this was what was wrong with the current systems and why effective services were still unavailable.

In summary, the committee said, the only way our organization could *really* be on target, *really* understand the problems, and *really* come up with appropriate solutions was through heavy involvement in the organization of the minority groups. Anything short of this was simply do-gooderism at its worst. So, all that we had been experiencing in the civil rights movement, but which we blindly did not apply to our own efforts, was coming home to roost. The way to be of service is to provide power to those who are powerless so that they can then articulate their needs and have a central voice in determining how those needs will be met.

Most of the well-known voluntary agencies have been *providing* service to people in need. Some are now moving to use some of their power to try to interpret the needs of clients so that effective public systems of care can develop. Both of these efforts are commendable; but adequate pursuit of them necessarily depends on involvement of the target group in deciding what is important to do.

The most exciting associations, new and old, are those which are properly comprised and are focused on advocacy. The best of these organizations recognize that the ultimate outcome of the advocacy efforts is *empowerment,* i.e., securing power for the target group so they can effectively represent themselves. This is when *power to the people* takes on its greatest significance.

Let me provide a brief illustration which may help to separate the three levels of providing services, representing clients, and empowering.

Several years ago I was on the board of a family service agency at a time when that city's public welfare system was literally coming apart. I was dismayed to see that despite the chaos surrounding us, the agency's board meetings were still totally devoted to examination of the direct services of that one agency. Finally, some of us were able to persuade the staff and board that we had to use our knowledge of human needs, community organization, and the welfare system to influence the creation of a humane and sensible public welfare program. I recall that the board was amazed at how quickly we were able to have influence in doing this. They had overlooked that we at least knew something about the system, while most of those trying to improve it were quite in the dark. At that stage, we were moving from a preoccupation with *service* to the use of our special knowledge to *represent* those in our constituency who were welfare clients.

We recognized even then, however, that we were still a giant step from more effectively involving welfare clients in their own destinies—a pretty basic community organization principle which, however basic, we community organizers have constantly to relearn. Our next step, then, was to form parents' and neighborhood groups and to increasingly use these consumers as the spokespersons for the family service agency's point of view about welfare. We were beginning to move toward empowerment.

RECRUITMENT

If effective service and advocacy depend on involvement, where do you start? Obviously there has to be a realistic commitment and my experience sadly teaches me that that commitment has to be backed up at least in the formative stages with a quota system. By now I don't think there is an argument about the horrors of quota systems I haven't heard. They're undemocratic, discriminatory of themselves, abhorrent to a free society, and on and on. There's only one thing good about them—they make us do the job. There is no issue that more heatedly involves a board than the matter of quotas, but in the end organizations usually choke them down because, after all the arguments, we recognize that unless there is some rigid goal and annual evaluation, we just aren't going to produce.

The National Board of the National Association for Mental Health was given three years to achieve a 20 per cent goal for the Executive Committee and the Board of Directors, and it became policy that local groups should move as rapidly as possible "to mirror their communities." There is an annual survey and a report to the Voting Membership and to the Board of Directors. Frankly, I favor a fixed percentage for the local units. Even though "mirroring the community" may be the ideal profile, I think a fixed percentage is at least a first step. It gives the total organization a much more specific standard and a much sharper measurement.

Incidentally, one of the arguments we heard most often against substantial involvement of ethnic minorities and the poor was that these individuals would not be able to help in our fund raising. It is true that there are many doors which this group can't immediately open, but it has been my growing experience that the United Way, foundations and many special givers will actually respond more readily to the organization that is so comprised. Also, as I pointed out in a previous chapter on fund raising, the overwhelming proportion of dollars contributed in this country come from persons with annual incomes under $15,000. I also pointed out early in the book that nickel-and-dime and payroll deduction fund raising are really the base of support of most voluntary associations in this country. The fresh leadership which minority representatives provide allows us to spread our fund-raising base even farther and to bring into the organization some vibrant people who can "tell it like it is."

I'm always somewhat mystified and, I'll admit, perhaps a bit skeptical, when I hear people say that they agree entirely with the goal of representation and they even subscribe to the quota system, but they just don't know how to find the people to fill the quota. My feeling this way is probably unfair because, as I'll admit, it's hard to break down patterns and habits and it's hard to take a big enough step away from the problem to see it in logical perspective.

If people really mean to fill the quotas, it won't take awfully hard work to locate good people. Start by talking to minority persons who are public officials, ministers, teachers, representatives in other community organizations, and in the health and welfare departments. Talk to the leaders of the organizations representing minority concerns such as the Urban League, National Association for the Advancement of Colored People (NAACP), Congress of Racial Equality (CORE), the A. Philip Randolph Foundation, Black United Front, Spanish Alliance, Welfare Rights Organization, and so on.

You will find that many of the most active leaders are appropriately preoccupied with causes even closer to their own minority concerns, but by following this process you will find people who are sufficiently able and interested to join up.

Staff recruitment is no different from other aspects of fulfilling the commitment. It won't happen unless there is absolute determination. You have to make up your mind that that's the way it is going to be and just do it.

Shortly after the Mental Health Association quota system was voted, a job as department head of one of the four national departments opened up. There were logical people in the organization to be promoted into that post. There were also many other brilliantly qualified people who were immediately recommended. The only way I could reserve that job for a minority representative was to absolutely close consideration to anybody else. My resolve was challenged several times by the availability of exciting white candidates. Also, I learned I didn't know where to look for good minority candidates. The process was slow and I was discouraged. I talked personally or by phone with more than thirty minority leaders whom I knew or who were called to my attention. I was impressed at how easy it was to get to talk to these people even though many of them were significant community or national leaders. In the end, I found a very talented person who has done the job as well as it could be done.

Let me share with those of you who may be doing some recruiting, one thing which I learned and which I think is significant. When I am looking for an important staff person, one of the things I routinely put store in is the individual's work record. Within this I am careful to see if the person has at least stayed in each post a reasonable length of time, something like three to five years. This has always suggested to me stability, commitment, ability to get along and to stick with it. I was at first put off by the resumés of many minority persons because they had not this kind of career record. However, as I began to struggle with the search, I was impressed that people whose judgment I respected would speak very highly of candidates whose work record automatically suggested job jumping. The lesson I finally learned was that the opportunities for growth had been coming thick and fast. This, combined with the sort-term nature of many of the agencies and assignments, automatically dictated a fast shift in positions. Unless I had learned this lesson I would not have hired the person I did who has now been on his job for more than five years.

IT'S GOING TO BE DIFFERENT

If you're an average board or staff member, you will assume that "having done so much good by involvement of many minority representatives, they should be grateful and should now settle into the organization." You'll hope that this part of the struggle is behind you and that things can go on as usual. If that turns out to be the case, you will have picked the wrong minority representatives. The right ones are going to bring about some very real changes. They are going to bring a different perspective, a different determination, and a lot of questions. They are not going to blindly accept on faith the organization's existing directions, policies and programs. No matter how frustrating you find it and no matter how impertinent you view it, be prepared for the fact that your new recruits have learned the hard way not to passively accept whitey's precedents and policies.

They're also going to bring a different perspective and a fresh point of view along with a determination to exercise both. Their life-style has had to be different and they're satisfied that it's taught them some things and ways that are better than your approach.

You will have to accept that these new friends come to you with some skepticism about your motives and sincerity. They don't have to prove themselves to you nearly as much as you have to prove yourself to them. Be prepared for their impatience—they've had all the runarounds and have learned that the way you do something is to do it and to hell with policies or feelings.

You probably won't be prepared for their higher thresholds for argument and difference. The emerging leaders will tell it like it is and they're much more used to some pretty straight rapping, which I predict, you'll learn to like although initially it may offend you.

They'll probably be sufficiently uneasy and suspicious that they'll want to touch base with themselves to compare impressions. For example, don't feel that a Black Caucus is just a vehicle for disruption. It's more often a means by which the long excluded come together to feel at home. It's one of their ways to get a handle on what you're all about.

It's going to be different and, as long as you *really* do want to enlarge and enrich your representation, most of the difference is going to be for the better. But don't start down the road if you really want the status quo, and don't expect that your values have to become their values. Maybe many will, but new members have got to work it through for themselves. Also, many of them are going to bring suspicion and a sensitivity which will quickly respond to the conscious and unconscious prejudices and discrimination which you'll come to realize are pervasive.

If you're the administrator or president, do all you can to minimize the problems, including providing, if necessary (and it usually is), some sensitivity training for you and your people so that you can better recognize your own prejudices and the expressions of them.

One of the delicate balances early-on is whether the

organization and the minority representatives view their role as representing minorities or assisting in the over-all pursuit of the agency's objectives. This is not nearly so easily answered as it might seem. In fact, the minority representatives will want to be both and will have to be both. The minority figures will want to help the agency be responsive to the needs of their people, to help build bridges for even greater involvement, and to be certain that the agency is indirectly, if not directly, contributing to the elimination of prejudice and discrimination. On the other hand, they will resent being thought of as primarily black or Hispanic. The dual role will create an ambivalence for them and an awkwardness for the organization. This is a fact of life that can't be done away with, but which, when understood by all concerned, makes the situation more comfortable.

It is important that the organization provide minority representatives with across-the-board responsibility and participation so that they are not always assigned to tasks which emphasize the minority identification.

KEEP YOUR MISSION IN FOCUS

I mentioned in the beginning that most of the lessons I'm trying to learn relate to the problem of how to effectively reach and involve minorities. I also mentioned that one of the lessons I'm learning is that the organization has to be careful not to lose its own unique focus. Let me quickly acknowledge that there are some minority people with whom I've worked and many with whom I've talked who disagree strongly with these statements.

I argue, for example, that the basic role of the National Association for Mental Health has been the same for sixty years: to improve services for the mentally ill, to improve

attitudes about mental illness, and to work for the prevention of mental illness. I have constantly pointed out how
much these tasks need to be done and that we are the
citizens' organization responsible for accomplishing them.
I point out that our initial statement on minorities stated
that it is "glaringly apparent that among the poor of our
nation, serious illness, including severe mental illness, goes
largely unrecognized and untreated," and further stated
that "we view these facts with grave concern and resolve to
add to our current program a greatly increased emphasis
on the needs of those for whom the problems are the worst
and the services the least. These efforts will not require a
new program for the association, but will require determination to tackle the harder jobs first."

I hate to recall all the uncomfortable confrontations
I've had with minority representatives and others who
argue that if the minority representatives in the organization and in the community say that garbage is the problem
or housing is the problem, then that is where the National
Association for Mental Health has got to be. They argue
strongly that we've got to start where the greatest problems
are and then work from there to assignments more typically
related to our organization.

My position is that we have a moral responsibility to
lend our voice to the efforts of those groups which are
organized to deal with the other social ills which tragically
befall minorities. For instance, I think it is incumbent upon
the organization to make absolutely clear the mental health
implications that are so much a part of discrimination,
unemployment, underemployment, poor housing and the
rest, but I flatly state that the Mental Health Association
cannot desert the neglected cause of mental illness which
looks so desperately to the organization for relief and solutions. I argue that our job is to see that mental health

services are available, and because the need is greatest among the poor (and to the minorities who are so greatly over-represented among the poor), our service to the poor is largely performed through this route.

I've had some pretty angry people try to argue me down, stating that my position is simply a cop-out and that unless agencies like ours put all their resources into the fight against the social ills facing our country, there aren't going to be any agencies and there isn't going to be any country in the future.

Standing up to that kind of individual and to that kind of argument isn't pleasant. The more you get into this area the more you'll find that many minority leaders have found that the way to turn you around is to try to scare the hell out of you. That is why it's so essential to decide right from the start what you mean to do, and to have this in realistic balance with the basic mission of the organization. With that behind you, you will be in a position to know where you must bend and change and where you have to hold the line.

Don't be afraid to be humble in the face of the evidence for change. But also don't be pushed into going beyond what you believe in your heart of hearts to be right.

14.
Dealing With
Controversy, Dissent and Disruption

IF you're not involved in a good deal of controversy and dissent, you probably are not in the thick of things. Today most organizations dealing with vital public problems face a great deal of both internal and external controversy and dissent. It is likely, too, that such organizations are occasionally faced with disruption. Controversy of this dimension usually involves the uprising of people who feel their rights are not being protected—people such as racial minorities, women, youth, and homosexuals, or groups who believe they are badly underrepresented in the political arena—such as ethnic neighborhoods, ethnic political organizations, metropolitan areas or even consumers.

DEALING WITH INTERNAL CONTROVERSY AND DISSENT

Annual Meetings and meetings of the Board of Directors should be viewed as healthy arenas for controversy. If the issues are laid out in advance, well formulated and clearly presented, and if sufficient time is available for debate, then it is healthy and constructive for Voting Members and board members to question, debate and disagree.

One of the characteristic faults of voluntary organizations is that the leaders strive for compromise and for unanimous votes. My experience has been that if you are dealing with real issues, striving too hard for compromise and unanimity may mean you are not squarely facing the issues themselves or else you don't have the right mix of people, or perhaps you've watered down the issues until they're harmless and impotent. It's far healthier to have a split vote as long as the issues are on the table, the debate is fair, and there has been enough time for consideration.

Creating fair and objective consideration is easier said than done, however. Those in charge of the meeting often have strong feelings about the issues. Meetings are usually too short for any real discussion and there is too little advance dissemination of the facts to prepare people for adequate debate and vote.

If there is significant controversy, the organization must take the time to get the issues out before the Board of Directors or Voting Membership so the matter can be decided without any feeling that something has been put over on people. There will always be the temptation to slip a touchy matter through to avoid hurt feelings or ill will, and there will be all sorts of opportunities for parliamentary sleight of hand. Don't tolerate any of it. Be absolutely sure that a proper process is available and that this process is objectively and fairly followed to the letter.

It's better to lose even on critical issues as long as the organization comes out of the battle with greater confidence in the integrity of the process. It's also better to take additional time for debate and decision on major items rather than trying to put them behind you. For instance, on a major issue I almost always suggest that the matter should initially come up for reaction and discussion without a vote even though this means postponement. It strikes me as more conducive to correct decision-making and to confidence in the system to take extra time for consideration and review. Even on lesser issues I generally favor having the board consider issues at one board meeting for vote at the next. Committee chairpersons and staff members are almost always dismayed when I recommend this process. Usually they've worked hard on a project or on guidelines or a position statement and they feel that it's imperative that the vote be taken as soon as possible. My approach is that if the matter is so important, it's worth being sure that people know the issues. I also believe that with this course there is more likely to be followership once the vote is taken.

The posture of the leadership should be one of patience, tolerance and flexibility. I include flexibility because leaders will often have their own biases and yet they especially must be willing to seek out and really hear new facts and differing opinions. The more important the issue the more intense the feelings and debate are apt to be. You will find that some people will dig in their heels very early and will be adamant about a given position. You will also find that people tend to describe the issue as a matter of principle or moral right. Generally, if you look closer you will find that people have confused policies with principles or rules and regulations with philosophy. It is helpful to delineate the important distinctions between philosophy, principles, policies, procedures and rules and regulations. It's easy to take something lower in the order too seriously simply by confusing it with a higher value.

The executive director should not try to be the trial lawyer on every issue. Unfortunately we tend to emotionally identify ourselves as plaintiff or defendant and are in the middle of issues that don't really require it. As a result, we become more controversial than necessary and we tend to get too upset and too scarred. In an organization that truly has a capacity for controversy and dissent, you'll generally find that the executive director has a high tolerance for both and is more involved in maintaining an arena conducive to healthy controversy than in trying to personally win on every issue. I don't suggest a profile of timidity or passiveness, but I don't think it's healthy for either the organization or the individual when the executive director is expected to fight or even stand up and be counted on every issue.

Presidents are more likely to have a responsibility to support the chairpersons on current issues. They should be careful that the chair itself does not represent a bias and, particularly, they should not view it as a formal vote of no confidence if the decision goes against them.

At times, a controversy can divide the president and executive director, and, if not handled well, this can lead to an even greater problem than the original controversy. Hopefully, the president and executive director will be mature enough to work out their differences or at least be willing to agree to disagree and to have their different points of view presented for consideration and decision. It is especially to be hoped that maturity will allow each to handle defeat when necessary. I rarely disagree publicly with a president, but I do make it very clear to each new president that I have a right to do so. On those rare occasions when we do disagree and can't work it through, I always suggest that we work together in presenting the issue to the board. Fortunately, I've never run into a situation when it was not possible to follow this arrangement. I do know, however, that in several other organizations, even with the most talented and mature presidents and executive directors, there have been occasions when the two officers have found themselves locked in controversy. In such cases it's useful to have a third party explore the issues and present all the facts to the governing body. This process can also be useful if the controversy involves other factions in the organization, and it's particularly valuable if the differences have reached the personality level.

One of the frequent tragedies of controversy is that the staff becomes badly split. It's natural for the volunteers involved to want the backing of the staff people with whom they most closely work. When things reach this level of controversy, I insist that the staff stay out of it. Once a year I review with the staff the basic ground rules of our staff responsibilities. My operation could generally be described as the loosest tightest ship or the tightest loosest one. There are very few rules, but those which do exist are inviolable. One of them is that I am hired by the board to handle the staff operation, and that all the staff members are hired by me to help me do the staff job. People who know my operation generally see the side that provides tremendous delegation and latitude. But the staff and I know that the quickest way to disaster is for the staff to begin to publicly take opposite sides on issues which are seriously splitting an organization. Volunteers should not contribute to this by expecting, or trying to get, some staff members to take their side in the controversy.

When I have an honest disagreement with a department head, both positions are almost always put forward for decision by higher authority. However, unlike the rights an executive director has in relation to the president, department heads don't have a similar right to present their views regardless of the executive director's wishes. In that respect, the two jobs are not the same. The executive director is hired by the board and is ultimately responsible to it. Therefore, he has an obligation to provide his opinion to the board. The department head is hired by the executive director to assist him to carry out the staff job. In the very rare, bitterly contested matter, it may be very important that the executive director represent the singular staff voice.

There have been very few situations in my experience when it wasn't easy, natural and obviously the right thing to do to have the staff's differing views brought forward. It is basic to an executive director's authority, however, that if a management viewpoint is to be expressed, it must be the director's decision that is presented. Any worthwhile executive director is going to have able and strong people around him, and before expressing a management view he's going to draw fully upon that talent. When an obvious consensus can't be reached, even if he comes down hard on one side he's almost always going to see that the different arguments are made known to the board. But if, from his unique perspective, he should conclude that one staff recommendation is what's needed, that must be honored as a firm decision with no room for other staff to undercut the recommendation or the authority.

When any really major controversy is put before the Board of Directors or Voting Membership, a professional parliamentarian should be at hand. The parliamentarian should not be a member of the board. The person chairing the meeting should do everything possible to get the group to be willing to put the issues out for full and adequate debate before the parliamentary maneuvering begins. Despite the good intentions of Robert's Rules of Order, their implementation often thwarts early consideration of the broad issues. Someone's always too quick to jump in with a motion to amend, motion to substitute, motion to split and all the other maneuverings which so often focus debate either on the parliamentary procedures themselves or on issues which may not get at the heart of the matter.

Once the matter has been decided, the volunteer and

staff leaders must help the organization to quickly adjust to the decision and get on with the most positive aspects of the agency's program and operations. A good organization, like a good organizer, spends its time on issues which it can do something about and doesn't waste time on issues it can't do anything about.

Obviously peacemaking should be the order of the day, but once in a while it's not the best course to follow. Occasionally, it's better that people lose and move out of the mainstream. There is a great temptation in voluntary organizations to make up and to bring Charlie back into the chairmanship or to the Executive Committee to show him there are no hard feelings. This is usually the right thing to do, but sometimes it only perpetuates the underlying difference which was finally settled. There are times—not often to be sure, but there are times—when it's better to let some people fall away or go away mad. This may not seem fair, it may seem cruel, it may seem a contradiction to the kind of spirit that voluntary organizations try to generate, but some people and some controversies are better moved out so the organization can concentrate on what the clear majority wants to do. Remember that an organization can only sustain so much controversy.

This same caution should be a guide for people who want to shake things up. Volunteer organizations, more than any other kind, get shaken up very easily. Don't start too much controversy and dissent unless the board clearly believes a total shake-up is necessary. Otherwise, pick your spots carefully and move only on those matters most in need of revision.

Differences, debate, controversy and dissent can all be healthy and are a characteristic of vibrant citizen organizations. The organization and its structure must represent a healthy arena for the adversaries to have at it. The executive, in particular, must have a stomach for difference and an awareness that his larger job is to maintain the healthy arena rather than to personally take on each tiger as it comes along.

HANDLING INTERNAL DISRUPTION

One of the newer forms of painful controversy involves the internal disruption. This can apply to a board meeting or more likely to an Annual Meeting. A group representing minority members or a program interest within the organization may, for example, surprise the organization with a list of demands. There has not been enough experience to provide very good guidelines for this situation, but it does seem that there are certain common-sense approaches which should be considered.

For one thing, the meeting leaders should recommend that the agenda be changed to hear the list of demands. A reasonable time limit should be placed on this and, hopefully, it will be agreed to by both sides. At the conclusion of the time, the meeting's leaders should suggest that the organization's top officers meet with the faction to work out a timetable for early and sincere consideration of the demands. If the disruptors insist on control of the meeting, the matter of further change in the agenda should be submitted to the full body. If the full body is willing to continue the discussion and to deal there and then with the demands, that's their business. If they reject further discussion, then the intruders have to be asked to leave or else to be silent. If they will do neither, then the meeting should be adjourned for a certain period of time and during the intermission every effort should be made to work out some accommodation which doesn't compromise the organization or the vote of the members.

If all of this fails and, when the meeting is finally reconvened, the smaller group continues to press its demands, then the meeting leaders, with the vote of the full group, must decide whether to adjourn again or whether the integrity of the organization sadly but necessarily requires that the intruders be removed. I've never known a situation to reach that extreme, but the plan has to have some end in sight. It is more likely that reason will prevail and the officers will then quickly move to deal with the demands.

HANDLING EXTERNAL DISRUPTION

If you are dealing with a vital area of public concern, there may be times when outside groups will attempt to use your meeting as a platform for protest or when they may wish to disrupt your meeting with the purpose of either influencing the organization, gaining publicity, or presenting their outrage to your membership directly. This disruption by outsiders may be more difficult to handle than that generated from within. It may be hard to achieve a rational response because the outside group may be viewed as critics of your members or the group's charges and behavior may create a hostile reaction among your people. In either case, my advice is still the same. Keep your cool and handle the situation with as much common sense and good judgment as you can possibly muster. This will be a lot easier to do, however, if you've thought about these situations in advance.

Demonstrations, picketing and even disruptions are common forms of free expression. Because several organizations have been targets of demonstrations, it is appropriate to anticipate such an occurrence and to prepare for it.

It's good to act on the reasonable assumption of an open and orderly society and not to adopt a siege mentality. For these reasons, one should take formal advance precautions only when there is reasonable evidence that disturbances are likely. When such evidence is apparent, local authorities should be given specific information as early as possible. It's best to give this information personally to a superior police official. At the same time, it should be made clear that you do not seek to interfere with any legal demonstration, but only seek to protect the safety of your own volunteers and staff and to assure their ability to carry on the business of the organization without interference.

The basic approach should be that demonstrations are allowed, but they should not significantly interfere with the business of the organization. This point of view should be communicated to the members and guests when demonstrations are anticipated. One person should be designated as the security officer. He should be the person working with the police and hotel, and with any private security guards who are engaged.

People who will be leading the various sessions of the meeting should be informed and instructed. If there is real likelihood of picketing, demonstrations or disruption, all the participants should be so informed and should be advised on how to handle the various situations. Generally, picketing and demonstrations should be regarded without prejudice and certainly no member of the organization should try to interfere with those processes. It will probably also be useful to tell your members not to argue or debate with the demonstrators. This can only heighten already charged feelings.

If your session is a formal business meeting, then it is a closed meeting and you have a right to restrict access to the room. Generally, it's a sensible course to accede to a request of an outside group to present its concerns as long as there is an agreement that this will be held to a set period of time, preferably not to exceed 20 minutes. If necessary there can be an agreement that, at the close of that time, the members will be allowed to vote as to whether they wish to change their agenda in order to continue the discussion. The outside group should understand that if the members vote not to hear them or not to continue the discussion, that decision is final. If the demonstrators then move to disrupt the meeting, the session should be adjourned until the demonstrators have left or, if necessary, have been removed.

Removal is a harsh action, but if your members have assembled to do the business of your particular organization, and have had every opportunity to vote to change their agenda and do not believe it wise to further do so, then that's an aspect of freedom too. If possible, the meeting should be adjourned to another place or time so that the matter of removal does not have to be faced. However, in the extreme case, you must be willing to take that stance or the organization will be inappropriately intimidated.

If you are having a public meeting, then the situation is somewhat different. One useful device is for the citizens assembled in public session to agree on an agenda and to vote on it. If the demonstrators are already in the room and it is a public meeting, they have every right to also vote on the adoption of the agenda. If they win, then they can have their item discussed and those who want to stay can do so of their own choice. On the other hand, if the majority votes to adopt an agenda that covers the original purpose of the meeting, and the disruption still continues, then you can either just walk out, leaving the disruptors to carry on their own discussion or, in the extreme case, you can follow the same procedures outlined for the business meeting.

If there is any general rule, it is:

• Be willing to bend over backward to accommodate differences, but if the members are unable to proceed with their own meeting because of outside interference, don't be intimidated.

15.
The Role
of the National Office

If you are part of a national association it's absolutely essential to define the relative roles and mutual responsibilities for national and local operations. Under the best of circumstances there is rampant opportunity for irritation between the two levels of the organization. But don't invite those problems wholesale by not clearly identifying who should do what.

I like to start with an oversimplification which says that the national association provides supporting services to local chapters, where the agency's programs are carried out. This is an important place to start and it is where the focus should be kept. Otherwise, the many exceptions which of necessity exist in most organizations will tend to obscure the national organization's responsibility to help chapters.

IDENTIFYING THE DIFFERENT ROLES

Generally, the following considerations determine the roles of the two levels of the organization:

- *The local chapter's role is*
—to pursue the national association's program mission within the chartered geography,
—to secure funding for support of the program mission in that same area,
—to provide for support of the national operation.

- *The national association's role is*
—to provide support and services to chapters,
—to fulfill certain direct national-level responsibilities, *i.e.,*
  (*a*) Federal legislation and regulations,
  (*b*) interstate matters and communications,
  (*c*) staff recruitment and training,
  (*d*) service to national media,
  (*e*) liaison to other essential national organizations,
  (*f*) national meetings,
  (*g*) research,
—to provide dynamic leadership.

It doesn't matter whether your national office is organized as a corporate headquarters or as the hub of a federation, it is still the central office and, as such, must provide dynamic leadership for the total organization. This includes responsibility for the organization's spirit, direction, thrust, policies and guidelines.

KEEPING ATTUNED TO CHAPTER NEEDS

One of the basic ways to keep the complementary local-national roles operative and therefore to keep the national level attuned to local needs is to be sure that the National Board of Directors is comprised overwhelmingly of people who come from the local affiliates. Even if your organization operates as a tight national corporation, there can't be correct decision-making and follow-through without local volunteers having had a substantial part in making the decisions.

In an earlier chapter, the importance of proportional representation in the Voting Membership and of population considerations in the make-up of the Board of Directors were stressed. At the national level, the organization should be very largely peopled and run by individuals who have current, or at least recent, experience on the firing line. The local chapters must feel it's *their* national association or, no matter how dynamic the leadership, there won't be followership.

And even if you achieve ultimate representation, don't expect that harmony will automatically follow. You will still have to work hard at it. Remember Pogo's discovery: "We have met the enemy and he is us."

Don't become an Eastern establishment. When I was working in California it was very upsetting to be regularly told that there couldn't be more Californians on the national board and national committees because of the travel costs involved. We were putting up almost 20 per cent of the national budget, but still couldn't have proportional representation because the office happened to be in New York. That's not fair.

It's unfortunate but obviously a fact of life that national organizations do have many critical direct national-level responsibilities. These tend to blur the basic responsibility of service to affiliates and, almost automatically, tend to absorb an inordinate share of national interest and energy.

National staff and volunteers find it more fun to deal

with matters at the national level. Obviously, it's more fun to have a feeling of doing something directly rather than to be consulting with or assisting people who then will have the satisfactions of follow through. National-level responsibilities are also more visible and thus they tend to get the attention. For these reasons and more, it is an absolute maxim of national-level operations that the attention will rapidly drift toward the direct national-level responsibilities to the neglect of the primary responsibility of service to local affiliates.

One of the best ways to prevent this drift away from the primary responsibility of service to affiliates is to be certain that in your year's plan very specific activities are defined which relate to maintaining and expanding service to chapters. I try to be certain that *at least* 50 per cent of the national staff's time is devoted to service to chapters. Though I've been stressing this for several years, I can absolutely guarantee that if I let up on it for even six months, the next time I take a look the proportion will have dropped from 50 to something like 25 per cent.

It's interesting and also discouraging to note that this is just as true with people who have recently come to the national office from chapter jobs. Therefore, it is essential to develop administrative devices to lock in time for local chapter service. These devices should include a way, such as time sheets, to identify whether the activity relates to direct national responsibilities or to service to chapters.

A major step in meeting the responsibility for service to local chapters is to guard against the tendency to think of consultation primarily in terms of national staff. It's my own constant goal to hold direct national staff consultation to a minimum. National staff and officers should play a broker role: to help identify problems and aspirations in one chapter and to identify other chapters which have already dealt with those problems and aspirations and then, in various ways, bring the two together. It has been my goal (still far from achieved!) that in my national travel budget, travel for persons other than the national staff should come to better than 50 per cent of the total. This can dramatically expand the National Consultation Program. It's also a way of improving it. Local staff and volunteers are far better consultants and communicators simply because their credibility is greater and their experience much more immediate.

I've given a sign to every member of the national staff of the Mental Health Association which reads: *"What Makes Your Presence There So Essential? Use Volunteers and Chapter Staff in the National Consultation Program."*

There are a fantastic number of ways in which this kind of consultation can be provided. For instance:

National Officer Visits to Chapters.
Chapter Staff Visits to National.
Volunteer and Staff Visits to National.
Consultation with Other Chapters.
Staff Visits to Other Chapters.
Staff and Volunteer Visits to Other Chapters.
Special Meetings among Several Facing like Problems
　or with like Aspirations.
Attendance at National and Regional Meetings.
Specialized Staff Training.
Specialized Volunteer Training.
Regional and National Specialty Meetings.
Attendance at Staff Training Sessions.
Consultation from National Committee Members.
Consultation from Outside the Organization.
Participation in National Committees.
Intercity Meetings.

One other part of the National Consultation Program that bears watching is where the emphasis is given. Generally, and often of necessity, an inordinate amount of time is given to the smaller and often weaker units in the organization. This can lead to such an extreme that the larger units feel they are not getting adequate attention. The large units may not be clamoring for help (perhaps because the only thing you are offering is national staff consultation and the larger units aren't particularly awed by this!), but you will have to find ways to invest in your larger units or the organization will be in for trouble. I try to keep the fact in very clear focus that eight states comprise better than 50 per cent of the population of the country (California, Michigan, Ohio, Illinois, New Jersey, Texas, New York, Pennsylvania) and that 35 metropolitan areas have almost 70 per cent of the population. With this in focus, I work hard at ways to be certain that the national organization is assisting these large units with their problems and aspirations. Most often our assistance to the larger groups comes in the form of promoting and funding intercity consultation and meetings.

One of the keenest responsibilities the national level has involves the development of the organization's volunteers and staff. Fulfillment of this responsibility requires allocation of realistic time and money, along with meticulous follow-through to be sure that orientation, training and retention are fully attended to. The national office is automatically the administrator of the organization's career staffing program. Previous chapters of this book cover many aspects of this, but the subject is reviewed here to underscore the unique responsibility the national organization has for staff development. This includes recruitment, orientation, training, transfers and promotion, fringe benefits, and over-all development. The national level has a like responsibility in the area of volunteer development. This responsibility is not as clear or as easily organized as staff development and as a result this part of the job is usually neglected. The goal is to be certain that volunteers in the organization are given orientation, training, encouragement, and recognition, along with an opportunity for increased responsibility. The national office obviously can't do all of this, but it is responsible for the over-all design and to see that the job is being done.

SHAPE STRUCTURE ACCORDING TO FUNCTIONS

Just as there is an absolute need to clearly identify the unique and complementing national and local roles, it is also essential to determine what the organization's basic structure should be. Should you have state organizations? Should there be regional offices? Should the national office be largely centralized or decentralized? What size should the local chapters be?

The basic rule should be to keep it all as simple as possible. That is, I wouldn't have state offices unless they are absolutely necessary. I wouldn't have regional offices unless I were convinced this was going to do enough good to offset the additional bureaucracy which it would produce. I certainly wouldn't have a larger national office than is necessary.

On the question of size of local chapters, while it won't universally apply, my experience has been that a very active voluntary organization will have so many projects going that it will need at least one full-time staff person. This automatically dictates that the chapter will have to have an income of $40,000, which, in turn, suggests a population base of some 250,000 people. That's assuming you can raise between $.10 and $.15 per capita. In certain states or sections of states, putting that much population together spreads the area of a chapter unrealistically. In such cases, I generally favor having the area staffed from a central office.

It is terribly hard to generalize, but the three rules that generally apply are:

- Form should follow function.
- Keep it as simple as possible.
- Have a minimum dollar base for chapter status.

NATIONAL ANNUAL MEETING

There was a good deal said about the Annual Meeting in earlier chapters. However, the National Annual Meeting is such a very special creature that it deserves special mention here. It is the major vehicle by which national leaders can promote the spirit, thrust, camaraderie, and communication so necessary to the total organization. Too often the board and even the national staff tend to take the Annual Meeting for granted. We don't realize the responsibility and opportunity it represents and thus we don't set aside enough time to do it imaginatively and well.

Each year I talk with the national staff about the importance I attach to the National Annual Meeting and the kind of preparation I think is necessary to make it an experience people will go away from with new respect for the national association, new pride in the organization, and a tremendous storehouse of information to apply back home.

We go over our service plans to identify the problems and aspirations of our local units, to match people for meals and social functions in order to promote optimal communication and informal consultation. We set up our cocktail hours in a "cocktails and conversation" format so that people can go to specific tables to talk about subjects of interest to them. This not only breaks the ice—which it is so essential to do—but it also provides people with a good deal of information.

I'm sure it's the same with most national organizations, but the handbook governing all the technical arrangements is a heavy tome. In our own case, the manual starts with the selection of facilities and runs through several hundred pages ending with instructions on providing tips to hotel employees who have been particularly responsive. In between there is a collection of lessons learned which help make certain that our meetings are professionally and thoughtfully done so that people go away with a confidence that their national association is well run and does care about them. This, in turn, has instilled a greater spirit and commitment in our membership.

Not everyone can get to the National Annual Meeting and we tend not to realize how helpful it is for people to see the organization beyond the limits of their own chapters. Some national organizations don't any longer even have a National Annual Meeting. For instance, the Girl Scouts of America meets every three years. That organization uses the first of the intervening years for regional meetings, and the second for development and discussion of the issues which will be decided in the triennial National Meeting. I favor some such system because it plays up the opportunity and responsibility to hold regional or sectional meetings which will give many more people a feeling of being part of something special.

MINIMIZING FRICTION AND CREATING UNITY

You'll find that affiliates treasure their local autonomy and identity, but for publicity, fund raising and other purposes the organization profits from a nationwide identity.

Periodically, most national organizations go through a study of name change and usually the emphasis is to try to create a common identity. I recently did a review of the health and social welfare organizations which are members of the National Health Council or the National Assembly of National Voluntary Health and Social Welfare Organizations and it was interesting to find that the trend is clearly toward a common name. That is, local units are increasingly identified in the same way as the national board, but with some local qualifying identification such as "American Cancer Society, Pennsylvania Division." This satisfies the desire for common identity without obscuring the local tie.

Even more perplexing is the quest for a common program. Many organizations automatically have this, but many do not. And, in those which do not, there are usually strongly differing views as to what is the most important thing for the organization to be doing.

There is value, of course, in terms of identity, camaraderie, training and impact for the whole organization to be doing some of the same things at the same time. This can be the fund-raising campaign, a membership campaign or certain program thrusts.

It's good practice to have formal affiliation agreements between the national body and chapters. These agreements should make clear what the responsibilities of both parties are. I favor having an affiliation agreement run for three years with renewal subject to some formal evaluation of performance. The national organization should also be evaluated just as often.

There are abundant opportunities for national-local differences, friction upset, irritation and disputes. The volunteer leaders should recognize how debilitating this is and do everything possible to develop and maintain effective relationships. Serious differences should be worked out on a volunteer-to-volunteer basis. The organization's mission will be too important and your volunteering will be too precious to have the time taken up with acrimonious, unpleasant or unproductive relationships.

It's a cardinal responsibility of staff to do everything possible to minimize the chances of friction, but generally when there is a very significant relationship problem, it comes down to staff attitudes. A recent president with whom I worked reached this conclusion: "In a voluntary agency, the orientation and attitudes of the volunteer leaders almost exclusively reflect the orientation and attitudes of our executive directors. I am increasingly struck that it is almost an axiom that volunteer attitudes reflect staff attitudes. It is realistic to expect that some of this must always be with us, and therefore, the Association must do much more to work with the staff leaders to be certain they understand the implications of it. We must also, however, work much more to be certain that volunteer leaders themselves are given much fuller opportunities to know and understand the Association and current issues."

There should be some formal mechanism for handling a major dispute. This should be a standard part of the organization's policies. This procedure should be invoked only as a last resort, but not so late that it won't serve to avoid total breakdown. For instance, the policy might provide that the national body and the affiliate will, through various means, agree on the make-up and chairing of a Disputes Committee, which will either have final authority or will report to the National Board which will.

The financial support arrangement between local chapter and national organization should be fair but firm. The full Voting Membership should be involved in setting the authorization levels or financial formula, and significant adjustments should always carry with them a good deal of lead time for local accommodation. Adherence to the support plan should be absolutely required. There is nothing that breaks down an organization's discipline, morale or general relationships more quickly and certainly than a loosely observed financial support formula. If a catastrophe strikes a chapter, obviously you will have to bend, but it should be a situation reported to the full membership. It's a good practice to have loan funds to assist affiliates faced with difficulties. In this way, the pattern of support is not broken. Loan funds should be limited to a maximum of three years and hopefully on a sharply declining scale.

If some units arbitrarily begin to violate the support agreement, work like the dickens to interpret to the local leaders the consequences for the whole organization as well as the consequences for the local agency. Involve volunteers from sister organizations to help with the interpretation. If all this fails you should disaffiliate the chapter. At a certain point, the national body has to make it clear that, in fairness to the other units, arbitrary adjustments are not tolerated.

The object of all of the efforts to minimize friction and create unity is to use the wonderful volunteer energy and time to fight for the cause and not with one another.

16.
Evaluating Results

Voluntary agencies are usually so busy *doing* that there either isn't time or else it seems a poor use of precious time to become involved with serious evaluation. At some point, though, someone inside or outside the organization is going to want to know if the effort is reasonably successful. And then you'll be pressed to provide some justification and assurance.

A medical researcher, long active in voluntary agencies, has this wonderful description of how citizen groups generally evaluate their results: "Any group as bright as we are which has worked so long and hard as we have must have done a lot of good." This pleasantly cynical characterization of our approach to evaluation provides a mirthful caricature hardly to be believed, but don't dismiss it too hastily! When those doubting Thomases begin to raise questions, you may well find yourself reacting instinctively, and maybe even a bit testily, with a rather subjective "It must be the most obvious thing in the world that any group as bright as we are . . ."

There is always the possibility, however, that at some point this may not be good enough either for some members of the board or for some contributors, or even for yourself. You will then want to have some more objective measurement of whether it's all really worthwhile or whether at least you're getting all the results possible.

EVALUATION CAN BE EASY

Evaluation doesn't have to be complicated. It can be as basic as people deciding what they want to achieve by the end of the year and then figuring out later if they got there. At its simplest, evaluation starts with an attainable goal to be accomplished at a realistic date, with a prior commitment to be willing to stop what you're doing on that date to look back to see if your goal was actually reached. The sad reason so many organizations don't follow this simple procedure is that they don't even start out with a plan, and therefore they don't have a specific goal or a deadline to check back on.

My formula is:

• Fuzzy goals equal fuzzy evaluation and unfortunately the combination usually adds up to fuzzy performance.

In the chapter on Constructive Planning I said that much of the planning in our agencies is characterized by the commonly heard expression: "We're going to do as much good as we possibly can, and we just can't do any more." I also said that specialist planners have a way of making planning so involved that we tend to dismiss their recommendations as being beyond the resources and sophistication of our voluntary operation. The same thing happens, too, with evaluation.

Foil the experts! Don't start out to reduce all your options to mathematical equations, don't try to quantify your goals, and don't get talked into doing an involved program budget. All you really have to do is to be a bit more specific about what you want to have accomplished by when, and make yourself look back.

If what you see when you look back isn't pleasing, you'll automatically begin asking *why,* and this will be the beginning of a more effective marshaling of resources so as to be able to accomplish the things that really are most important.

At this point any planners reading this are probably tearing their hair out because their science has been stripped down to such nakedness. But, nevertheless, planning can be easy, and it can be simple. In the chapter on Constructive Planning I quoted the Peter Principle which says, "If you don't know where you're going, you'll end up someplace else." An evaluation sequel might be: "If you don't know where you've been, can you really be sure you were there?"

There should be a built-in mechanism for self-evaluation. As stated above, this can be as simple as at the end of the year taking a look to see if your goals have, in fact, been achieved. This is the most basic form of self-evaluation and should be a routine part of every organization's operations.

In addition, there should be some mechanism by which the board can take a fuller look periodically at the organization's operations and activities. For instance, this review should determine whether or not basic planning and evaluation are being done annually. You'll find that these, too, can be as simple or as complex as the operation itself.

Periodically—at least every five years—you should find some means to have an outside evaluation done. This is most easily arranged if you are part of a national organization. For various reasons, you may resist having representatives of a national board or staff come in. If that's the case, you can put together a team from your sister associations so that you're really having a peer review. An effective evaluation of any sort will depend, however, upon the degree to which measurable standards are at hand.

DETERMINING STANDARDS AND GOALS

The first step in evaluation involves knowing what constitutes acceptable performance. In the November-December 1964 issue of the *Harvard Business Review,* Earle Lippincott and Elling Aannestad published an invaluable article entitled "How Can Businessmen Evaluate the Management of Voluntary Welfare Agencies?" Their central thesis was that *if the basic organizational components of the agency are operating effectively, you can assume that the output is likely to be worthwhile.* They acknowledged that this isn't an exact equation, but they believe, for example, that if the board and the basic committees are functioning—including regular meetings with quorums present—it is *likely* the agency is not wasting its time.

The operating standards which Lippincott and Aannestad looked for included the following questions:

1. Are the board and staff set up to work effectively?

2. How well defined are the needs served by the agency and its program for meeting these needs?

3. Are adequate financial safeguards and sound controls maintained for fund raising?

4. Is the agency's work related to that of the national organization and of other planning groups in the field?

5. Is the agency doing a good job of what it is set up to do?

6. How many other agencies are trying to do all or parts of the same job?

7. Does the agency function in proper relationship to government agencies?

When I was with the California Heart Association, we took Lippincott and Aannestad's position two additional steps. We agreed that one can be encouraged if the basic operation seems to be functioning. We recognized, however, that this doesn't assure that the end product is really good or is even as good as it should be. Therefore, we added two elements. The first was to identify the basic activities which we believed a chapter of the American Heart Association should be handling well. Second, we acknowledged that one of the great things about voluntary agencies is their role as innovators. Obviously, then, certain activities couldn't be anticipated, so we gave a whopping one-third of the total score to those unusual things which the chapter might be doing over and above the basics.

As a result of this, the standards were then divided into three parts: (1) Basic Organization, (2) Basic Activities, and (3) Additional Activities. There was an evaluation of a chapter every three years by a peer group of representatives from other chapters. This had many intended and desirable results, but it also had the side benefit that those doing the evaluation learned a good deal about how to improve their own chapters.

NATIONAL BUDGET AND CONSULTATION COMMITTEE STANDARDS

The National Budget and Consultation Committee (NBCC), composed of 150 leaders from communities across the country, had the responsibility of evaluating and passing on the national office budgets of agencies which were part of the United Fund. (The function has since been taken over by the Committee on National Agency Support (CONAS), a direct unit of United Way of America.) The NBCC developed standards for national voluntary health, welfare and recreation agencies. Though the standards apply to the national agencies, most of them will have relevance for local organizations.

1. *Basic Organizational Requirements.*
   The agency must be incorporated, have adopted bylaws, and be organized and operated in pursuance thereof. It must:

   —be established and operate as a nonprofit, tax-exempt corporation, gifts to which are deductible by the donor for Federal income tax purposes,
   —operate in the health, welfare and recreation field.

2. *Voting Membership.*
   The Voting Membership exercising basic legal control of the agency should be defined in the corporate and related papers. This membership should be representative of the main interests in the agency's field of work. It should:

   —elect the Board of Directors, so that it reflects the will of the agency's membership,
   —possess the power of amendment to constitution and bylaws,
   —have an annual meeting, with adequate notice of and information about matters to be acted upon.

3. *Governing Arrangements.*

Governing arrangements should include at least the following:

a. A Board of Directors adequate in number to represent the main interests in the agency's field of work, meeting regularly, establishing policy, providing supervision of operations and finances, and serving without compensation.

b. A specified plan for turnover or other arrangements which provide for new members is essential.

c. There should be a minimum aggregate of four meetings annually of the Board of Directors or the Executive Committee, including at least two meetings of the board with average attendance of at least 50 per cent of their respective memberships.

d. In measuring the degree to which the board fulfills its functions, the nature of its deliberations as well as the activity of its members in operating committees and in providing leadership, interpretation, guidance and support in other ways should be considered.

e. An Executive Committee chosen from among the members of the Board of Directors which may act for the board during intervals between its meetings.

f. Additional committees to assure the performance of the main functions of the agency and to provide a sound basis for board decisions.

g. Provision for the election of officers, their terms, tenure and the filling of vacancies.

4. *Personnel Policies and Staff.*

The agency should:

—have a written statement of personnel policies, job descriptions and provisions for staff evaluation, formally approved by the board and made available to the staff, and

—employ an executive director and professional staff with qualifications appropriate to the agency's field of operations.

Agency policies should be established by the board and administered by the staff. The executive director should not be a member of the board but, with other staff personnel as needed, should attend board meetings and participate in the deliberations of the board and the formulation of policy.

5. *Need, Goals, Program.*
   The agency should operate in a defined area of need, should specify its goals and conduct its program to meet that need. Periodically it should reassess such need, goals and program. Conformity to this standard should be measured by such criteria as:
   a. Evidence of need.
   b. Definition of the segment of need served by the agency.
   c. Resources for a substantial program in the area of defined need.
   d. Maintenance of accurate service records.
   e. Understandings with other agencies in its field to prevent wasteful duplication.
   f. Projection of long-term and short-term program goals for specified periods, and a method of board review of achievements reached at the end of such periods.
   g. Ability and willingness to change or modify goals

and program in response to need and public interest, and in cooperation with appropriate planning agencies.

6. *Budget.*
   The agency should:
   —operate on an annual budget under defined procedures of budget preparation with board examination and formal adoption,
   —control expenditures by such approved budget, with significant departures permitted only by authorization from the Board of Directors or Executive Committee.

7. *Support Plan.*
   The agency's financial planning should annually:
   —assess and specify financial expectations as to source, amount, and equitable distribution of support,
   —use a support plan based on the preceding which, in the light of previous experience and current conditions, sets forth a reasonably dependable method for obtaining the income budget for the period under consideration.

8. *Nondiscrimination.*
   An agency which exists to serve people generally should not determine the availability of its services or the membership of its board or staff by considerations of race, religion or national origin.

9. *Cooperation with Tax-Supported and Other Voluntary Agencies.*
   The agency should maintain relations with tax-sup-

ported and other voluntary agencies in or related to its field of services. This would include:

—registering research and demonstration projects with pertinent information exchange centers and making appropriate use of resulting information,

—clarifying respective roles and relationships of voluntary and tax-supported agencies working in the same field,

—participating in national planning bodies,

—recognizing the obligation not to make substantial alterations of major program functions without consulting other affected agencies.

10. *National-Local Relationships.*

The agency should establish such relations with local communities as the nature of its work requires.

a. All agencies (whether or not they have local units or community-centered programs) should:

—initiate local fund raising or services only after consulting community planning and fund-raising bodies and existing related agencies as to need and arrangements,

—maintain relationships with these local planning bodies, and with state and local public bodies having planning responsibility, in cooperation with its local units where these exist, or directly if there is no organized community unit,

—maintain channels by which local views and needs on program planning, fund raising and other matters of concern may be transmitted to the national agency,

—provide for the maximum degree of local autonomy consistent with national-local charter or affiliation agreements.

b. Agencies with local units should in addition maintain:

—affiliation or charter agreements which specify the relationship between the national agency and the local unit, outlining the structure, services and financial operation of the local unit together with the responsibilities and accountability of the national office thereto—such agreement should be available for review by appropriate planning bodies,

—adequate arrangements for seeing that the local units fulfill the charter or affiliation requirements and, depending on the type of agency, for the provision of such services as program leadership, standard setting, counseling and evaluation of local operations

11. *Education Program.*

The agency's education program should have valid content beneficial to significant audiences. This program and its cost should be differentiated from promotion publicity for fund-raising purposes and its cost.

12. *Fund Raising and Promotion Publicity.*

The agency's promotion publicity should adhere to ethical standards, such as respect for clientele and factual accuracy regarding needs served, character of services offered, the volume provided, and other accomplishments. The agency should follow accepted practices of fund raising and should comply with applicable legislative requirements. It should not mail unordered tickets or merchandise with request for money in return, solicit funds from the general public by paid telephone solicitors, or enter into arrangements to raise funds on a commission basis. It should make honest disclosure of fund-raising costs to contributors and the general public.

Fund-raising costs, including those of related promotion publicity, necessarily vary from agency to agency, but in general should not exceed 25 per cent of the funds raised per year in the first five years of operation nor 15 per cent of such funds per year thereafter. In judging whether an agency's fund-raising costs are correctly stated and reasonable, factors to be taken into consideration should include the extent of public understanding of the agency's work, factual justification of costs, and the use of sound accounting practices.

13. *Financial Management and Accounting.*
Generally accepted standards of financial management including the bonding of persons handling finances should be adhered to.

The agency should have its accounts audited annually by independent certified public accountants, whose examination should be made in accordance with generally accepted auditing standards. The audit report should include:
a. Financial statement showing all the agency's income, disbursements, assets and liabilities, together with changes in endowment and other funds, reserves and surplus during the period, all in sufficient detail to be in accord with sound accounting practices. It is emphasized that all items in the foregoing categories, which are under the agency's ownership or control, must be included in the financial statement.

b. An auditor's certificate in the conventional form developed by the American Institute of Certified Public Accountants.

The agency should participate in efforts to develop systems of accounting in cooperation with representatives of contributors, other agencies and the general public which will work toward comparability of items from agency to agency. When a system of uniform fiscal reporting has been developed which is acceptable to the accounting profession, agencies, significant contributor groups, and contributor reporting services, the agency should adhere to it.

14. *Public Reporting.*

The agency should make annual program and financial reports to its membership and the general public. The financial report may be in summary form, but must be consistent with the audit report. The agency should respond to requests for detailed information on any aspect of its operations or program from any responsible source.

15. *Evaluation.*

The agency should have an orderly plan for periodic evaluation, whether by staff and board arrangements, outside consultants, or a combination of these. While it is to be expected that evaluation will be a continuing function of administration, formal evaluation should be undertaken periodically by the board in order to review program in the light of current needs and in terms of the agency's stated purposes, specified goals, and relations with other agencies in its field, especially tax-supported agencies. Also, the agency should cooperate with independent evaluating bodies in an effort to provide an objective report for the general public.

OTHER AGENCIES' STANDARDS AND EVALUATION

There isn't room to include the standards, checklists, and affiliation criteria of several national organizations. Much good work has already been done in this field, however, and certainly those of us who are seriously determined to develop comprehensive standards and an evaluation process should seek to learn from the experience of some of the following national agencies:

- *The Volunteer Bureaus of America* have a very good outline for "self-appraisal of a Volunteer Bureau."
- The *YWCA* has a very sophisticated and comprehensive set of "standards of excellence" which cover constitutional responsibility, administration, program, and community relations. Within each of these categories there are scores of sub-items designed to gain a very clear and exact picture of how a local YWCA is operating and what its program is.
- *The Easter Seal Society for Crippled Children and Adults* has developed a useful "checklist" for evaluating a local unit. The original intent of this checklist is described in the Foreword: "Easter Seal Societies across the nation have often expressed a need for a simple consolidated checklist of organization and administrative procedures." That checklist has been greatly expanded and now constitures the Society's "Performance Report."

At the very least, an organization should plan by writing out what some of its goals for the year are, and should evaluate by taking a look to see whether those goals were accomplished. The experience will lead toward more realistic goal-setting, the presentation of those goals in measurable terms, and a more careful analysis of why some goals were not fully achieved.

Despite the fact that planning and evaluation can become exceedingly sophisticated and complicated, they start with the basics of articulating goals, establishing timetables, and looking back at a later date to evaluate the progress or lack of it.

EVALUATION CAN BE SOPHISTICATED

Planning and evaluation are obviously vital management skills which, in complex operations, will need to be carried to very sophisticated levels. The only reason they were stripped of some of their status earlier in this chapter was to make the point again that most things boil down to common sense, and if people can start there they actually will get started.

For larger and more complex organizations the planning and evaluation process will require specialist skills in order to take advantage of the refined methods which have been developed for more scientific examination and determination of goals, the quantification of these goals, and a very exacting evaluation which automatically identifies the impediments which stand in the way of maximum fulfillment of goals.

In the years when he was Secretary of Defense, Robert S. McNamara and his fellow Ford "Whiz Kids" brought planning and evaluation to a high level, and their schemata have been further refined and applied throughout the Federal government up to and including the human services agencies.

In the future, organizations which wish to secure government contracts and grants to provide services to people will find themselves required to present their objectives and goals in mathematically-defined units of service, providing indications of dollar cost per unit and human value per unit.

United Way of America has published a manual, "UWASIS," (United Way of America Services Identification System) which is designed for use by local Funds so that all programs supported by United Fund dollars can be evaluated in terms of the units of service offered per dollar expended. Here, too, the units of service will be quantified, both in terms of dollar cost and human value.

The seemingly cold and calculated approach by the Federal government and others to an appraisal of relative human needs strikes many people as substituting scientific procedures for moral judgments. At some point, however, someone has to be able to provide a clearer picture of which programs can have what impact on what degree of human suffering. Hopefully these facts will be served up to thoughtful, sensitive human beings who will also exercise humaneness in making value judgments about human needs. At least this will be an improvement on the irrational approaches which have so often been used for identifying priorities and supporting programs.

There are many today who argue for an even higher level of planning for human services. René Debós has called for the "development of social goals." He decries the piecemeal "ad hoc approach to solutions to human problems" which, he says, is no longer tolerable. He believes it is no longer appropriate for scholars to avoid a coordinated centralized approach to long-term needs and their solutions on the old grounds that individual scientists must be left unencumbered. In essence, Debós believes that we should not be asking, "Where is science taking us?" but, instead, we should rather be asking, "How can we manage science so that it will take us where we want to go?" To do this, he says, we first need to decide our social goals. As an example of a sound goal, Debós suggests that by the year 2000 we may have decided that it should be routine for all persons to have a 100-year life span including an opportunity for health and happiness. Along this same line, U.S. Senator Walter Mondale of Minnesota has several times introduced legislation in Congress to develop a National Social Report which would more exactly define what basic social goals we as a nation should establish. These approaches are obviously designed to better articulate relative social needs. An integral part of the effort is to define the goals so that specific programs to achieve them can be developed and an evaluation of progress and results will be possible.

For many, the process and mechanism of developing a program budget are basic steps to planning and staying on target toward accomplishment of goals. But providing comprehensive information about a sophisticated program budgeting approach would take a book of itself. To give some firmer grasp of what's involved, let me quote from a section of the United Way of America's "A PPBS Approach to Budgeting Human Service Programs for United Way." (This statement is attributed to Paul A. Permer. It originally appeared in Permer's "Planning-Programming-Budgeting Systems—Its Concepts, Characteristics and Objectives.")

"PPBS is a framework for planning—a way for organizing information and analysis in a systematic fashion so that the consequences of particular choices can be seen as clearly as possible. It attempts to do three things: (1) to display information about the functioning of actual programs so that it is possible to see easily what portion of resources is being allocated to particular objectives, what is being accomplished by the programs, and how much they cost; (2) to analyze the costs of alternative methods of achieving particular objectives so that it is possible to rank the alternatives in terms of their relative costs; (3) to evaluate the benefits of achieving objectives as comprehensively and quantitatively as possible in order to facilitate the setting of priorities among objectives.

"Under the PPB System, the six major elements of a program budget are: (1) an attempt to describe the programs in narrative statements involving a statement of objectives and a breakdown into sub-programs and targets; (2) a breakdown of budgetary allocations by functional programs which involves crossing organizational lines when necessary; (3) an attempt to identify and quantify the results of the programs; (4) a relation of output to input in terms of cost-benefit analysis; (5) a relation of programs to total resources in terms of a discussion of alternative methods and priorities; and (6) long-range planning, generally from three to five years ahead."

Whether evaluation is approached by setting some goals to be accomplished in a set period of time and then looking back to see what happened or is approached by the most scientific means, it still comes back to the simplicity of defining goals, relating the resources to achieve those goals, and then, later, determining if the goals were in fact reached.

PROFILE OF EFFECTIVE VOLUNTARY OPERATIONS

One quick way to evaluate your organization is to match yours against a profile of effective voluntary operations which I developed after years of trying to figure out why some voluntary organizations failed and others succeeded. The successful ones had these characteristics:

- A cause worth getting excited about.

- An ability to generate funds to do the job.

- Programs that could in fact do something for the cause.

- Adequate attention to morale in order to keep the undertaking spirited and vigorous even when the immediate tasks were not.

- Appropriate emphasis on increasing the number of citizens who would become involved.

- Ability to keep the volunteers in charge even after the operation was staffed.

- Flexibility to respond effectively to new problems and opportunities and to fit the profile of "ad-hocracy" which must increasingly characterize the useful ongoing organization.

- A capacity to keep the real mission in focus no matter how frenzied things became or how great the pressure was to move into new areas. This means that all important decisions were made with the organization's reason for being kept clearly in the forefront.

- Vision to see beyond the horizon, along with sensitivity to really feel human needs, plus an almost contradictory toughness to build an organization capable of translating the vision and sensitivity into change.

Afterword: Keeping
Voluntary Organizations Independent

We as a nation are blessed with what seems to be a nearly unanimous view that voluntary participation in public affairs is badly needed. Everywhere there is a pervasive realization that we need a pluralistic approach to our problems. People whose political orientations are markedly different realize that government alone cannot solve all our problems and that maximum involvement of people creates good government and provides a fresh way to tackle public problems. Thus, it is only natural that many people want voluntaryism to be vibrantly alive. There is reason to fear, however, that we may smother the voluntary movement with our concern. The more attention turned in this direction, the more we tend to want to structure the nongovernmental sector, with the result that the genius of spontaneous citizen action is submerged. Instead of pursuing the basic jobs of protecting and promoting the freedoms of assembly and speech so that citizen initiative can flourish, we tend, with our unfortunate American penchant for orderliness, to overdefine voluntaryism and then legislate and regulate its development.

There are problems developing which will have serious consequences for the voluntary sector and thus for the country as a whole. Various laws, regulations, practices and proposals are emerging in this country which would greatly restrict the right of individuals effectively to organize themselves. These include: (1) the increasing number of local and state ordinances which give authorities the means to narrowly define which organizations may solicit funds, thereby limiting opportunities for reform; (2) tighter definitions on tax exemptions which greatly restrict an organization's efforts to influence legislation and regulations at a time when one of the greatest services of the private agencies is to interpret public needs to government officials; (3) forced compliance with an IRS uniform accounting system so involved as to be beyond the grasp of many emerging organizations; (4) some local United Way efforts to centralize control of voluntary activity are doing so around a basically conservative orientation; (5) Congressional proposals to punish universities which are considered too liberal in allowing student activism; (6) proposed Federal restrictions on public interest law firms, and (7) proposed and actual changes in the tax laws which will have serious impact on giving funds to private causes. These and other moves are designed to provide "neater" organization and operations among the existing pattern of private agencies, but their great harm comes in inhibiting the development of new groups which may be the unpopular but necessary instruments of tomorrow's reforms.

If, in our many new efforts to legislate voluntaryism, we are to serve the future well, we must start with the broadest possible frame of reference as to what constitutes healthy citizen participation. If the new laws and regulations reflect a narrower and dated frame of reference, the results will unintentionally (but sometimes intentionally) be repressive to the important categories of activists which are excluded. There is no greater danger to the preservation of our democratic form of government than to allow those in power to have any great say over who the reformers might be. It is dangerous to forget that much of the best volunteering in this country has involved the rabble-rousing Patrick Henrys, Jane Addamses, and Dorothea Dixes of other times whose unpopular efforts reformed child-labor practices, prisons, mental hospitals, and the corruption of "leaders" of their times.

The central issue is that citizen participation in public affairs is a concomitant of free speech and assembly, and if we are too eager to control certain kinds of activism we may restrict the very freedoms which are the avenues by which peaceful reform may take root in the future.

It must be hoped that all those concerned with the promotion of voluntaryism in this country will increasingly devote themselves to the basic question of how we can maintain the freedoms which give rise to citizen action.

Most of what one says about the nongovernmental sector points to heterogeneity rather than homogeneity. About all one can offer as a common attribute is that these agencies represent citizens rallying voluntarily around causes and primarily using private contributions to finance their efforts. Beyond that, any description becomes diffuse: *100,000 tax-exempt organizations pursuing 1,000 causes in generally uncoordinated fashion, often with conflicting purposes and philosophies, with no central voice or clearinghouse, with a vast range of motivations, skills and effectiveness, and with such myriad conceits that characterization itself is unwelcome.* One should not view this complex colossus with dismay, however, but with an appreciation of the composite value of the effort and of the freedom which prompts it.

In an essay entitled "The Nongovernmental Organization at Bay," Alan Pifer, president of the Carnegie Corporation, regrets that in the voluntary movement there has "never been a concerted initiative for the creation in Washington of a single voice to speak for the interests of the nongovernmental organizations field, a voice such as that provided for higher education by the American Council on Education." He continues, "Perhaps, given the diversity of the field and its lack of integration, this is the way it has to be, but the result is a babel which amounts to no voice at all."

Yet the real contribution and impact of voluntary associations must be the influence of millions of voices in their own organizations and communities. The total of all these separate voices contributes far better than any one voice to our democratic symphony.

In a response to Pifer I said: "If we have a point of difference within our more important agreements, it would seem to relate to what I sense is your wish that the process of voluntaryism and nongovernmental activity might be made a bit more orderly. From my side I worry that in cutting the diamond, the real source of brilliance, the million separate lights, may be sacrificed."

One of the most urgent issues facing voluntary agencies today is whether they should accept substantial government funds to sustain and expand their programs. Voluntaryism is a process, born of freedom and necessary to freedom, so diffuse that it accommodates the extremes of our national aspirations and so grand that it includes the disparate pursuits of a thousand different programs. Government's role in promoting voluntaryism should be devoted primarily to the always difficult—but always essential

—preservation of the very freedoms which allow such activities to flourish in the first place. Intermediate efforts to subsidize voluntaryism, however well intended, will likely have the reverse effect because they will reduce the clear degree of conviction, responsibility and independence required of the voluntary sector. Dollar support must, to some degree, reflect philosophical or political prejudice, which brings discrimination to the very arena where it least belongs. It is significant how often important citizen efforts begin as rebellious and unpopular dissensions or exhortations. Some of the most important contributions of the nongovernmental sector have been in this category. I wonder if it is practical to suppose that any governmental organization would not be prejudiced toward such groups.

At a time when our national aspirations and our available funds are often outdistancing the capacity of our institutions to keep pace, there is clearly a need for stoking up all appropriate machinery. In our eagerness to expand the contribution of the nongovernmental sector, however, it is essential not to undermine the principal long-term values of independent agencies. My experience tells me that long-term government support of any agency or complex of agencies tends to create a quasi-governmental entity with decreasing value as an independent force.

Unless an agency consciously moves into such a quasi-governmental status, there should be a strong inclination against sustaining governmental grants. Adding 25 per cent to the existing budgets of nongovernmental agencies won't add much to the total expenditures from all sources, and adding more than 25 per cent presses the nongovernmental organizations toward too many compromises.

The constantly growing demand for program efforts is so great that the government cannot get the job done alone now or in the near future and a partnership of govern-

mental and private agencies receiving substantial government support may be essential. In this case, government
and nongovernmental agencies will have to make decisions
about organizational and financial relationships that will
have a profound effect on the nongovernmental sector,
particularly on the current and future role of individual
agencies. Also, we must recognize that to some degree we
will be obscuring the role and responsibility of government
itself for meeting many of these needs.

A new program partnership in a quasi-governmental
setting is also a way of extending important usefulness.
There may be a great swing of many, if not most, of today's
categorical agencies over to the quasi-governmental setting. In fact, we are already witnessing the development of
a whole new level of public agencies operating on general
or specific contracts, using volunteers and having freedom
of day-to-day activity.

It is essential to be aware that creating quasi-governmental organizations that are viewed as outside the immediate spectrum of formal government tends to obscure
the role and essentiality of the truly independent sector. As
we move into such an arrangement, it is vital to recognize
and appreciate that we will then in reality have three kinds
of organizations—governmental, quasi-governmental and
independent—and that it will be the independent agency
which will continue to be our principal source of objective,
noncompromised and truly independent opinions.

In a recent editorial in *Journal of Current Social Issues,*
editor Paul H. Sherry presented this view:

"Their [the voluntary agencies] role is not primarily to
serve as an alternative to government, but, instead, to help
keep government honest and responsible. The primary
role of voluntary associations in American life is to continually shape and reshape the vision of a more just social

order, to propose programs which might lead to the manifestation of that vision, to argue for them with other contenders in the public arena, and to press for adoption and implementation. For a voluntary association to do less than this is to abdicate its civic responsibility."

There are, obviously, multiple roles which the independent agency can play, but anything which compromises its independent voice in public matters diminishes its capacity to function in the role society most depends on it to perform.